MY OWN DEVICES

MY
OWN
DEVICES

True Stories from the Road on
Music, Science, and Senseless Love

DESSA

DUTTON

DUTTON

An imprint of Penguin Random House LLC
375 Hudson Street
New York, New York 10014

A version of "Daylight in New Orleans" appeared in *The New York Times Magazine* as
"Wandering New Orleans After Seeing It from the Stage," March 21, 2017. A version of
"Going Empty" appeared in *The Art of Wonder* (Minneapolis: Minneapolis Institute of Art,
2015). Sections of "A Ringing in the Ears" were posted and broadcast by Minnesota
Public Radio, June 14, 2013. A section of "How Hockey Breaks Your Heart" appeared in
Minnesota Monthly as "Dessa's GMO Dilemma," March 18, 2014. Sections of "Slaughter #1"
appeared in *Black Warrior Review* as "The Crossing," March 2013.

DUTTON and the D colophon are registered trademarks of
Penguin Random House LLC.

LIBRARY OF CONGRESS CATALOGING-IN-PUBLICATION DATA
Names: Dessa, 1981– author.
Title: My own devices : true stories from the road on music, science,
and senseless love / Dessa.
Description: New York, New York : Dutton, [2018]
Identifiers: LCCN 2017061172 (print) | LCCN 2017061527 (ebook) |
ISBN 9781524742300 (ebook) | ISBN 9781524742294 (hc)
Subjects: LCSH: Dessa, 1981– | Rap musicians—United States—Biography. |
Singers—United States—Biography.
Classification: LCC ML420.D479 (ebook) | LCC ML420.D479 A3 2018 (print) |
DDC 782.421649092 [B]—dc23
LC record available at https://lccn.loc.gov/2017061172

Printed in the United States of America
1   3   5   7   9   10   8   6   4   2

Set in Bembo Book MT Std
Designed by Cassandra Garruzzo

Contents

CONTENTS

MY OWN DEVICES

Up on Two Wheels

I started rapping seriously, if inexpertly, at about the same time I fell in love (also seriously and inexpertly). I did both with the owner of a Ford Festiva. If you're unfamiliar with the model, it's a cartoonishly small car. Imagine a large black man, dreadlocks tied in a blue bandanna, and a ponytailed brunette beside him; add cup holders and a stick shift, then laminate those people. That's a Festiva. And that was us.

He was a chain-smoker, former drummer in a hardcore punk band. I was a chain-smoker, former valedictorian. He rapped with a group of guys who called themselves Doomtree; their CD featured a line drawing of a dead bird with Xs for eyes. I'd just started making music and I thought the stuff he produced was strange and incredible; he recorded performances that I would have scrapped out of hand as imperfect—vocal takes where he forgot a line and giggled, where his voice broke, where he was nearly out of breath. His songs didn't sound like the product of an artist in a big studio; they sounded like the proof of a person in a big feeling. He conducted even little, daily tasks in ways that would have never occurred to me. When I saw that he'd entered my number into his phone under *eff oh echs,* I asked, "What does that mean?"

"You'll get it."

I thought for a moment. "I don't."

He laughed. "You're a fox."

At twenty-two, being loved by him was one of the best feelings I'd ever had. Now, single at thirty-six, and having traveled the world many times over, not too many feelings have compared.

I'd grown up in South Minneapolis as a brainy middle-class kid. When I was a girl, my parents called me Chatty Cathy—a nickname derived from a doll popular during the sixties with a pull string on her back, who emitted a constant stream of chatter until the string rewound. My mom says I announced my first real life goal from the throne of her office chair: "I want to have a conversation—you know, where I talk, then you talk, then I talk—but all about the same thing." In grade school I was skinny, headstrong, but still eager to please. When I hit fourteen, dark moods started to cycle through. I cut off my long hair and walked down to the riverbank to dye it pink in the Mississippi. I started drinking and dressing as a boy; I ran away from home and slept outside for a few days, woke up fully clothed under a hedge to discover I'd started my period. Wearing a Lakers cap pulled low, gas station clerks called me *sir* when I paid for the candy on the counter. I nursed coffees at the Hard Times Cafe, a sanctuary then for happy anarchists, busted-ups, and punks. "Just so you know," the barista said, then reached beneath the counter to lift up a stack of posters with my face on them. My mom had papered the city, but the barista assured me Hard Times wouldn't hang them; I was safe there. It'd be a decade later, in a Saint Paul psych ward, that I'd learn there was a word for those moods, and that they often linked to menstrual cycles. But they were intermittent through my teens and I kept my grades up, managed to stay clear of any real trouble. By the time I went to college, I was brunette again. I studied philosophy, attracted by the imaginative depressives who spent their workdays debating the design of the world. I finished my coursework in three years with honors, leaving with a degree, a functional angst, and a burning ambition that wasn't affixed to a particular objective. I knew I wanted to devote myself completely to something—I wanted to be like the stressed-out lawyers on TV dramas who paced through the night with loosened ties and take-out boxes. I wanted to be considered a success and I wanted to be on the right side of a hard fight. But I wasn't sure what job or even what field to pursue. I was carrying a jet engine under my arm, looking for a plane.

Meanwhile, the boy who'd eventually drive the Festiva did his growing up in an apartment unit, with a devoted single mom. He was a smiley, round-faced kid, with catlike, almost-black eyes. His dad split when he was six. He loved his mother effortlessly and absolutely, but had an irrepressible independent streak even when he was very small. Once, locked in the closet by a cousin, he managed to attract an adult rescue by banging against the door, his little muffled voice shouting in the dark, "You can't keep a black man down!" At fourteen, he got his first tattoo—leopard print on his left shoulder. He spent his teenage years skateboarding, learning to play bass, then drums. He recorded his bands onto cassettes, carried a rat in his pocket, did enough drugs to swear off them for a while, and eventually got expelled from high school for distributing anti-prom propaganda.

We spoke for the first time on the steps of The Playhouse, an arts compound in Uptown, Minneapolis. I was there visiting a friend, Yoni, who lived in the building. Although it's since burned down, The Playhouse had twelve bedrooms, a recording studio in the attic, a slide that went from the second floor to the basement, and an iguana that I remember as the sole occupant of one of the third-floor units. Yoni had recently invited me to join his band, a hip-hop outfit where I'd be one of three rappers. Initially, I'd been hesitant to accept. I knew how to write essays—I'd taken writing classes in college—and I had a good singing voice—I slayed Sheryl Crow and Fiona Apple at karaoke—but I'd never rapped before. Yoni had extended the offer based on the strength of a few pieces he'd seen me perform at a poetry slam. Fuck it, I figured, it was exciting to be asked. And I needed a place for my jet engine.

I was sitting with Yoni on the cement steps, mid-cigarette, when the Festiva pulled up. It was summer, late afternoon. The little car parked across the street and a two-hundred-pound man stepped out, dressed entirely in black: dress shirt, shoes, bandanna, slacks—much too hot for the day. "Coming from work," the man said by way of explanation.

"What are you, a ninja?" I asked.

He was a friend of Yoni's, it turned out, and they went in the house to chat.

As soon as they were inside he asked, "Who's she?"

He made me a mixtape of rap songs. On our first date, we drank whiskey under a bridge. He left me little notes in his tiny lowercase script that said, *i like your face* and *if we're careful, we could do this for life.* I slept at his house most nights, listening in on the 3 A.M. recording sessions in the basement. I went to all of the Doomtree rap shows, sweating along with the other fifty attendees at a grimy basement club. Each member of the crew had his own brand of charisma; they were funny and angry and impulsive and a little bit sad and their show was always one second away from falling apart completely—like they were rounding a corner, up on two wheels, for the whole set.

During the day my boyfriend and I rode around running errands in the Festiva. He kept a long list in his head of the people he knew and the things they might want; this index allowed him to barter for items that he himself wanted but couldn't afford. He knew, for example, that the clerks at the record shop would be hungry mid-shift. He knew that his friend at the sandwich shop could hook up free meals when managers weren't around. So if he gave the sandwich friend free passes to the next Doomtree show, he could get some bagged lunches, which he would then deliver to the record shop in exchange for a copy of the limited-edition twelve-inch that hit the shelves yesterday but cost more than he had on hand. He didn't feed meters. He signed his credit card slips *Punk*

Rock. He broke every rule—with a flourish. And everyone seemed to love him in spite, or maybe because, of it. I'd had boyfriends before, but falling in love with him felt like converting to a new worldview—where almost anything was possible and almost nothing was mandatory.

In the car, he played me all sorts of underground hip-hop: Vast Aire and Sage Francis, acts signed to indie labels like Def Jux and Anticon, and local groups like Traditional Methods. He played some hardcore punk too, from bands with names I can't remember. My formative experience as a rapper happened in his Festiva, idling in the parking lot of an Old Country Buffet.

He was behind the wheel, I sat shotgun. He put a beat on the stereo. "Alright, rap."

"Man, I really don't want to do this." I hadn't written many lyrics yet and was painfully self-conscious about performing them in front of someone so good.

"You gotta just do it."

"I'm too shy with you right here."

"Okay." He opened his door. "Roll down your window a little."

He left the car, came around to my side, and started pounding a beat on the metal roof above my head.

I started a verse, quietly at first, then louder.

He listened through the cracked window.

When I was done, he got back in the car. It was good, he said. He thought I had real promise. But, "Why don't you rap like you write?"

My rap verses were mostly just lightweight wordplay. My essays, some of which he'd read, were different: they had extended metaphors, literary allusions, subtext. It had never occurred to me to try to write rap like that.

Later, back at the Doomtree house, he helped me count bars properly. There are two snares in every bar, he explained. Then he explained what a snare was.

The first Doomtree producer to let me write a song over his production was MK Larada. He was one of the more reserved members of the group, with fair hair, a sharp tongue, a blazing intellect, his own frequent dark moods, and a slight tic when he was onto a strong creative idea. He became one of my closest friends. Drinking into the early hours of the morning, we recorded a song that would be called "Hawks & Herons" in the Doomtree basement. I realized I'd fallen asleep at the microphone only when my beer hit the floor and woke me up.

Within a year or so of meeting them, the Doomtree guys sat me down in their living room. In a sea of crushed cans and brimming ashtrays, they officially asked me to join the group. This did not feel like a job offer; it felt like being asked to join an expedition that would last many years, maybe my whole life. They were my brothers now and I was their sister. Giddy, I called my mother to share the news. She asked what a Doomtree was. I told her. She warned me to watch out for cocaine. "*Mom.* We don't have any money for cocaine." We could barely afford flyers.

Maybe because there are no major labels based in Minneapolis, a DIY ethic prevails. Doomtree didn't have a manager or a publicist or a booking agent—not all of us even had phone numbers. So Lazerbeak handled the money; Sims sorted out merchandise manufacturing; Paper Tiger and MK Larada designed the CDs and posters; I helped write artist bios and press releases. We all met once a week to scheme on the next big show or recording project.

Today's conventional wisdom says that the best way to live a life is to keep all the components partitioned—love, money, friends. You're not supposed to date your boss, or go bowling with your analyst, or borrow large sums of money from your drinking buddies. We think of ourselves as a store-bought cake with a sheet of wax paper separating all the slices so that they never touch: neat, single servings.

But hanging out with Doomtree, it was all one thing—social, professional, romantic. I did all of it with the same people and often at the same time. There were no hobbies and no off-hours, no work-life balance; there was just writing songs and walking to SuperAmerica for cigarettes and drafting set lists and drinking with the guys and making album budgets and goofing off and collapsing into sleep tucked into the leopard print of my boyfriend's left shoulder. None of it came apart from the rest.

On stage, we were still a mess, and that was part of the magic. Someone was always bleeding into his microphone or trying to catch the mixer before the bass rattled it off the table and crashed it to the floor. The precariousness of the live show was like a watermark that proved to the audience it was all real: we hadn't rehearsed these moments, choreographed these feelings—that was not a staged fall, that was just a fall-fall. I sweat through my clothes with the rest of the guys, full of whiskey and adrenaline and youth and anger. Stage was a place for all of the outsized feelings that didn't fit neatly into daily life. You can't scream in love or fury in line at the Walgreens pharmacy; you can't roughhouse with grown men at the post office; and you can't calmly explain to your parents that you'd rather sleep outside, under a stranger's hedge, than in your own bed. But with a little songcraft, those dark moods were perfect grist for performance—we rattled up the biggest feelings in one another, and anyone else close enough to hear.

We started getting some good press, building a decent draw. While the whole group often performed together, we played and recorded individually too. Everyone was both a member of the crew and a solo artist. My boyfriend released an album, strong enough to get picked up for rerelease by a larger label called Rhymesayers. Soon his rate of ascent started to outpace the rest of ours. He was getting real gigs, more money, legitimate interviews in shiny magazines. He started touring regularly, and landed a spot on a full North American routing, where he got to travel on a tour bus with a couch and video games in the back. He was gone for many weeks at a time. And was excited to be away.

Back in Minneapolis, I was earning some accolades too. But I still wasn't supporting myself on music, and there was no clear indicator that I ever could. Rappers are like violinists or gymnasts: they start when they're knee-high and they're famous before they can rent a car. In my midtwenties I was old enough to be a *retired* rapper, moving into comedic movies.

Earnings from a handful of concurrent part-time jobs covered rent and spending money. I waited tables, did some tech writing, and painted faces while dressed as an enormous butterfly. Like a meteor shower, a series of questions flashed through my consciousness at regular intervals:

Q: How long should I do this before I give up?

Part of the challenge in becoming an artist is that you have to place your bets before you're fully dealt. You have to assess your talent, still half-formed, and decide what you are willing to stake on it.

There's no best-practice handbook for the pursuit of unlikely dreams. How much of your life should you spend trying to be an astronaut or a fashion model or a professional rapper before deciding it's time to redirect your energies? A year? Two? Ten?

Some members of Doomtree are genuinely art-for-art's-sake creative types. Cecil Otter is like that, I think. He'll emerge from a thirteen-hour production session bleary-eyed and blissed-out by whatever he heard through the headphones. I've never been that kind of purist. For me the *communication* of an artistic idea is fundamental to the endeavor. If there wasn't someone at both ends of the line, at some point, I'd just want to hang up.

Q: What are the opportunity costs here?

I knew that I was capable of making a good living in another field—I had gotten good grades, could interview well, was willing to work hard. If music *wasn't* going to be my life's path, then the time I spent writing songs and bios and press releases might be better spent doing something else—going back to school, or applying for a full-time job, or maybe teaching English abroad, where at least it'd feel like I was contributing. I was a lousy waitress. I was a pretty good tech writer, but couldn't envision it as a long-term gig. And I couldn't butterfly forever.

Q: Am I delusional—like, fully out of my damn mind?

I'd venture that there are thousands, maybe tens of thousands, of young women at this very moment who aspire to be the first female president. And one of them will be. The problem is it's impossible to tell if you're the one.

When small children say they want to be quarterbacks or tap dancers, they're applauded for their audacity. Aunts and uncles toss a ball around the backyard and buy a little fedora for Christmas. When you are a grown-up who says she wants to be a rapper, the blush is off the rose. The conversation at the Christmas table is more likely to include the words *compound* and *interest* than *follow* and *dreams*.

And it *is* a little crazy to believe that you can navigate a career path that seems to pan out so rarely. The numbers say you're almost certainly wrong.

Q: Could wanting it badly enough make it real?

This question isn't about hard work—that's a prerequisite. It's about taping blinders to your temples; categorically writing off the critics who don't like what you do; categorically writing off the counsel of the people who love you and worry about how you're doing, to insist, *I am going to will this into reality.*

This is the Tinker Bell model. She's only real because she is clapped into existence. The children refuse to entertain any alternative, and the force of their desire and their determination has metaphysical consequences.

The Tinker Bell model is the nuclear option. It taps every reserve. It permits no Plan Bs. It's bold, reckless, conceited, juvenile—right up until it works. And then, in hindsight, it's brave, windblown, and scored with strings that sustain right into the commercial break.

I've known artists who've tattooed their hands and faces to ensure they'd have no recourse, no desk-job escape chute.

I started painting faces when I was fourteen. My dad's second wife, Linda, taught me how to do it. She was petite, quirky, and irreverent—a skilled botanical artist who ran a talent agency for children's events. She taught me how to mix paint, meticulously trained me on each design, and helped style my costumes. By the time my first EP came out with Doomtree, I'd been painting faces for ten years.

At the Renaissance Festival, I wore an enormous tulle petticoat beneath a hot-pink silk dress. The bodice cinched tight in the back with crossing laces (you could be fined for visible zippers). Occasionally, a wagonful of Renfesters would drive by and point at me as part of something called the Wench Tour.

During the Christmas season, I wore striped tights and a Santa's hat with an enormous spring inside, so that the white pom-pom bobbled above my head, even when I stood still as death beneath it. I could not pass through any doorway standing upright.

Corporate picnics were the bread and butter of the operation, however, and my normal work uniform was a short blue dress, bright red boots, pigtails affixed with holographic ribbons, and an expensive pair of butterfly wings. They were made with real feathers, hand-cut, painted, and layered to look like the scales of a monarch wing. Heading to work from the Doomtree house, I carried a Caboodles case full of paints in one hand and my wings in the other. When I arrived at a gig—sometimes at a public pavilion, sometimes at a theme park—I put my wings on in the car, before any of the kids could spot me.

In the face-painting line, children didn't censor themselves. There were sweet kids and there were assholes. There were boss kids and support-staff kids, and their talk was frank and constant. If children could unionize, that's where they'd have done it.

I don't buy into the hype about children as untrammeled innocents. They're seeded with all the human traits. Sometimes they share, even when they have less than they need. Sometimes they hoard, even when they have more than they want. They just don't have the resources for big projects. And they get tired early. But I *do* believe that kids warrant special consideration. They have big heads that goof up their center of gravity. They don't have properly formed kneecaps until they're, like, three. They haven't been in the rock tumbler long enough to have their curiosity and affection polished down. They'd ask me to marry their dads, just so I could come live with them. They'd rub my leg while I was painting, just to rub my leg. They'd fall asleep with their faces in my hand and I'd have to wake them up, reintroduce myself, remind them where they were, and then slowly turn a mirror to reveal the butterfly mask I'd painted while they were out. For someone who is not particularly romantic about kids, I take them more seriously than most people I know.

Sometimes while I was working on one, another would sneak behind me to reach out and lightly touch one of my wings. I'd shiver and yelp and she'd return to the line freaked out and excited, hissing, *I told you they were real.*

Most days, I fielded the same set of questions:

Q: Can I get two?

"Unlikely. This line is very long. But if there are no blank faces, come back and I'll do your other side."

Q: Are you a kid or an adult?

The costume made it tough to tell if I was a giant child or just a parent in disguise. "I'm an in-between."

Q: If your wings are real, then can you fly?

"Kid, nobody can paint while flying."

Q: Is this, like, what you *do*? Your *job*?

Well, honey, that one's complicated. Some days I paint faces. Yes, for money. And sometimes I write instructional manuals as an independent contractor. And sometimes I wait tables at a sports bar downtown. And sometimes I work as a temp for an agency like Dolphin Staffing—which is not as magical as it sounds—but at night, I am a rapper at a precarious point in her—

Q: I saaaaid, is this, like, what you *do*? Your *job*?

"Well, I'm face painting and you're waiting to get painted. So is that *your* job? Being second in line to get face painted? Are you a professional *paintee*?"

Q: Do you have a boyfriend?

I do, but only for a little while longer. He's becoming a famous person, I think, and there is no competing for first place in his heart because that position was already occupied by music-making when I met him. And maybe the best spot in my heart is reserved for the same thing. But all sorts of people want a piece of him now, including beautiful women who I don't think he has the self-discipline to turn away. And I am a sizzling mess: angry and jealous and vengeful and sad. That's the truth, but I can't share it with you because you're too young and this is supposed to be a party and I'm being paid by the hour.

Q: Do you have a boyfriend?

"How come? Are you single? Are you asking me on a *day-yate*?"

At indoor gigs, people walking by often bumped my table. That was bad news; a jostled table could slosh paint water, spill glitter. And a glitter spill is one of the worst things that can happen at a face-painting gig. Not because it was impossible to get out of the carpet, or because the rest of the kids lost their minds if they couldn't have any, but because the stuff was expensive. Even more expensive than our paint with real gold in it. We used a special glitter with rounded edges (gentler on the cornea, should it wind up in an eye) that had been subjected to laser light to refract holographically. In sunlight, the stuff was incredible. Linda, my stepmom-slash-booking-agent, sourced it from a special costume shop. She sold it to us in little jars, like a drug dealer in a ladybug costume.

One day, possibly jacked up on orange Crush and sheet cake, an impatient kid asked, "Well, can you fly when you're done painting?"

"I can't just fly from sitting still, I need a running start."

"But you flew here?"

"I did."

Dammit. That was a mistake, I thought. Lying to children gets convoluted quickly. Now at the end of the day, they'd all expect me to fly home.

Just as I'd feared, a gang of girls hovered as I packed up, all waiting to see how I'd leave. When I turned to go, they followed as far as they were allowed, watching. They wanted to know if I'd fly home—if I was the real thing—or if I'd get into some beat-up sedan and let 'em down like everyone else. Dammit, I thought. Dammit, dammit, dammit.

I'd told them I needed a running start, so I ran. I didn't know how long I'd have to go; I passed my car, figuring I could double back later. I was breathing hard. Then panting like an animal. My paints were banging around in my Caboodles case; my wings were bouncing on the elastic straps that held them to my back. I figured I'd run until they got tired of waiting to see if I ever made it off the ground. Or I'd run until I was too small to see. Or, fuck it, maybe I'd just have to run until they were all grown-ups, with their own day jobs, dreams, and disappointments.

We broke up. But we still performed together. During Doomtree meetings or before a show, I often felt queasy—being so near my *X* sent a rancid adrenaline through me. When I wasn't with him, I'd script elaborate conversations designed to punish him, and simultaneously to make him want me back. The amplitude of my bitterness freaked me out. Love can bring out the worst in people.

On tour, I smiled onstage and cried backstage. Hiding in the women's room of a club somewhere in America, my feet pulled up on the toilet seat, I could cry undiscovered for a long time. There was rarely another woman in the venue until just before doors.

On the road, a phrase like "I just need some space" meant moving to the back bench seat. It hurt to be near him, but leaving Doomtree felt unthinkable. The wider rap scene looked neither attractive nor hospitable. The world we had all built together was the only one I wanted to live in. The prospect of joining another crew felt downright outlandish; it would've been like losing your kid at the food court and being handed a different toddler by a mall cop—they're not *interchangeable*, man. It was Doomtree or bust. Or maybe Doomtree and bust.

Our tour routings had long stretches of back-to-back shows and grueling drives. Sometimes we'd push straight through the night to make it to the next club, or we'd pull over in a Walmart parking lot to catch a few hours of sleep before hitting the highway again. All seven of us passed out sitting up, wrapped in our coats in the winter, or sweating through our clothes in the summertime. One show at a time, audiences started growing.

A couple of weeks into a run, the public and the private melt into each other: you brush your teeth sitting on a curb in downtown Denver, nodding to passersby; you do a few yoga poses on the asphalt at the Amoco while waiting for the tank to fill; you wade into a roadside stream for some relief from the heat of the van before being chased off by a man yelling about municipal water contamination. The antics of musicians—their sunglasses at midnight, their handstands on barroom tables, their wasted hotel rooms—aren't just evidence of egos run rampant, they're also just the natural by-product of close quarters and protracted exhaustion: the grade-school loopiness of a sleepover that's been running for two months on vodka Red Bulls. At the end of a tour, the world has only three kinds of people in it. There are the people in your band, immediately identifiable at every gas station pit stop because they are also dancing half-dressed in the snack aisle. There are the people who come to shows, who are generally happy to be invited in on the joke. And there is everyone else—the civilians who are contemptuous of the way you and your cohorts are behaving at Perkins.

When X drove the van, I'd sometimes catch him looking at me in the rearview mirror, eyes soft with affection and apology. He was young, talented, sorry he'd hurt me, uncertain of whom to trust, and scared of being unveiled as a fraud. When he told me he still loved me I knew it was true. But I didn't trust him and I didn't know how to fix him. His childhood had left him over-hungry for affirmation and intimacy—and that hunger almost certainly helped make him such a force on-stage. It also probably drove his promiscuity. I couldn't afford to be tender, with him or with myself, if this show was going to stay on the road. While he tried to figure out what his life was becoming, I tried to figure out which spot on the bench seat couldn't be seen in the rearview mirror.

Slowly, I wrote and recorded my own full-length album. Many of the songs were about him. I tried to keep my nose down, cocoon myself in my work, and trust that I'd emerge with a record that would establish me as the artist I hoped to be. Part of me, though, was afraid I'd come out of the cocoon as just an older caterpillar with high-frequency hearing loss and a nicotine patch.

I called my first full-length solo record *A Badly Broken Code*, a line lifted from a Billy Collins poem. When the album came out, *X* invited me on tour. On a highway drive one afternoon, my phone chimed with a notification, then chimed again— friends were texting about something they'd heard on the radio. Within a few minutes, it was like I had a casino in my pocket: my phone was dinging constantly and *X*'s was lighting up too. Robert Christgau, a venerated critic, had reviewed my record on NPR. He'd compared me to famous songwriters like Joni Mitchell and Rosanne Cash, and, uncomfortably, also to *X*. It was an incredible endorsement—most of my reviews to date hadn't even spelled my name right.

If there was a single moment that felt like a pivot, it was that one: my phone buzzing in my lap and the prairie blurring in the windows. I didn't quit my day job in a defiant blaze of glory, but I felt confident that when I got back to Minneapolis, I'd eventually be able to hang up my wings. I could have never guessed, however, the lengths I'd go to find peace with *X*— professionally, romantically, and even neurologically.

Now, years after that first NPR review and my last face-painting gig, I'll sometimes stand at the edge of the stage during a Doomtree show. I'll put my finger to my mouth to quiet the room. I'll hold my mic off to the side, a gesture that will usually send a round of *shhh*s through the crowd. Unamplified, I'll yell something like:

"Hey, we're Doomtree. I'm Dessa. That's Sims, that's P.O.S, that dapper gentleman is Cecil Otter, and my guy Mike Mictlan is the hero who thought to grab the case of waters from backstage. Here behind the tables, where the magic happens, is Lazerbeak and Paper Tiger. If it's your first time seeing us: welcome. If you've been coming for ten years: thank you. The reason that seven musicians can play a two-hour show to a sold-out room—even though we don't have a big song on the radio, even though we aren't in Sprite ads, even though we write pop songs that are eight goddamn minutes long—is you. Our growth has been slow, and if you've been here from the beginning, you know that's true. But because we make our money in ten-dollar increments at that merch table right there—wave, Ander! That's Ander—we've been able to maintain total artistic control. We don't have to ask a record executive if it's a good idea to pick the song with a clarinet sample in 6/8 as the first single—*of course that's not a good idea*—but it's good art, dammit, so we're doing it. Doomtree runs on word of mouth and pixie dust. We are real because you've said we are. We're the Tinker Bell of this rap shit. So thank you.

"Alright, Paper, let's drop the next track. Here we go."

Glossary

Dessa: American recording artist. Type A personality, type O blood donor. Types sixty words a minute. Me.

Doomtree: A hip-hop collective based in Minneapolis. Founded in 2001, maybe. (Didn't keep great records then.) Known for genre-bending releases—blending rap, punk, pop, rock, and classical sounds—and an impassioned, physical live show that's part tent revival, part intramural hockey game.

Current roster: Cecil Otter, Dessa, Lazerbeak, Mike Mictlan, Paper Tiger, P.O.S, Sims.

Draw: The number of fans a performer can attract to a show.

"What's your draw?"
"A thousand at home, 250 on the road."

Day sheet: A detailed schedule of the day's events on tour, including drive time, phoners, time zone changes, opening acts, club Wi-Fi passwords, catering information, and set times.

"What time do we hit tonight?"
"Check your own damn day sheet, my guy."

Door deal: A show that pays performers a cut of the money collected at the door. Generally less desirable than a guaranteed fee.

Drop: Merchandise shipped from a warehouse or manufacturer to be intercepted by a touring party, to replenish their inventory on the road. Often addressed to a club or a hotel. Lost in transit approximately 30 percent of the time.

Ears: In-ear monitors that allow performers to listen to their live sound in earbuds, as opposed to hearing themselves amplified through speakers on the stage.

Femcee/Feminem: You do not need these terms. For anything. Ever.

Head: A rap fan well versed in hip-hop music and culture who identifies enthusiastically with both.

Hit the split: To draw enough fans to warrant a bonus at the end of the night. If and after show expenses have been recouped, an artist typically earns 60 to 80 percent of the profit.

Hype: Rap backup vocals. To hype another rapper's lyric usually means delivering that line in unison with the lead vocalist, often to allow him or her time to inhale.

Laminate: The laminated pass a performer wears to prove to security staff that he or she is part of the touring party and should be granted backstage access. Usually affixed to a lanyard, often threaded through a belt loop. Worn around the neck only by tour managers and nerds.

Midnight it: To set the knob on a sound console to zero so that the dial points straight up, like the hands of a clock at midnight. (I made this one up, and I think it's got promise.)

MOUNTAIN: The name of Doomtree's fifteen-passenger Econoline tour van.

One-off: A single show, not part of a routed tour.

Over/Under: A complicated betting game in which small amounts of money are won and lost based on the ability to accurately predict a bandmate's one-word answer to the question, "Overrated or underrated?"

> *"Okay, Paper Tiger: Divorce. Overrated or underrated?"*
>
> *[All passengers in the tour van quietly place bets on which he'll choose. Meanwhile Paper, in silence, contemplates everything he knows about divorce. He may consider the challenges of single parenting, private property law, the women's rights movement, the genetic foundations of pair-bonding. He'll then compare his assessment of the merits of divorce with the broader cultural appraisal—an impression he's gleaned from a lifetime of watching movies and TV, reading VICE and the New York Times, and conversations in bars and classrooms and on the train. He is strictly forbidden from offering any of his rationale.]*
>
> *"Underrated."*
>
> *[Paper shakes off his own private turmoil—who wants to say divorce is underrated?—while money trades hands. Now it's Lazerbeak's turn.]*

Spit a pella: To perform a rap verse a cappella. The rest of Doomtree argues that I invented this term, out of whole cloth. I did not. But I concede that it sounds dated and like it's trying much too hard—a description that sometimes fits me too.

Phoner: A publicity interview conducted by phone. While on tour, this type of interview often happens in a moving van, with bandmates listening in, mocking your answers, or talking whenever you're silent, pretending to be the interviewer on the other end of the line.

Punisher: A relentless fan who won't heed polite cues that a performer has other work to attend to. Rappers sometimes give one another discreet signals to indicate which members of the crowd are punishers.

Radius clause: A term in a performance contract that prevents a musician from booking a second show within a certain number of days and a certain number of miles from the first. Designed to consolidate draw and ensure that an artist does not book shows that might compete with one another. Very difficult to explain to old high school friends asking if you'll perform at their son's best friend's school's fundraiser.

Rat king: The tether-ball-sized knot of microphone cords that forms in the center of the stage as five rappers run around each other all night. Nearly certain Cecil Otter coined this one.

Ring the mics out: To test microphones for feedback and remove problematic frequencies. Part of the preshow sound check.

Spitter: A technical rapper, capable of delivering complex patterns at speed. (In Doomtree, Mike and Sims are, arguably, the spitters.)

Tour blues: Spells of sadness that hit either midway through the routing—when you sulk against the window with your headphones on for seven hours a day—or after you're home, where you have to do laundry at regular intervals and maintain human relationships and everyone confuses your job with a vacation which is insulting and you are exhausted and have what might be bronchitis and you've lost a lot of muscle mass sitting in the car all day and have blown out your knees by jumping on them as soon as you're out of the car and now that there's actually some downtime you're not sure how to function without the adrenaline baseline of living in a moving vehicle with the other Lost Boys.

Truth or Consequences: A municipality in New Mexico where tour vehicles are often stopped and checked for contraband, particularly drugs.

Van call: The time of day at which all members of the crew must report to the tour van for departure to the next city.

Walk-ups: People who purchase tickets at the door, as opposed to in advance of the show.

X: My ex-boyfriend. Depending on how you count, we dated on and off for thirty-two months or fourteen years. We've been in the same rap crew for most of our adult lives. We've been trying to fall out of love, and stay out, for a very long time. This is my side of our story. He was nice enough to green-light the telling of it. (He was, and is, a pretty remarkable dude.)

Breaking Even

Sometimes in the tour van, I do math in my head to kill the time. I'll calculate how many cashews I would have to eat per day if I were allowed only cashews (198), then calculate how many minutes would pass between each cashew if I had to eat them one at a time and at even intervals (7 minutes, 16 seconds), and then how many more cashews I could eat if I'd lived during the Rubenesque era, permitted to carry another twenty-five pounds of cashew weight. Sometimes I'll figure out the collective sleep debt of all the members of the touring party. Or I'll try to calculate how much extra gas we burn to haul the trailer, to haul our bodies, and to haul the gas itself before it's burned by hauling. Then we stop for gas. And I buy coffee and cashews.

A lidless Styrofoam cup of coffee must be tipped slightly when we pull into motion. This is intuitive, everyone does it: you hold the coffee away from your body, making a suspension system of your right arm, and you tip the cup in the direction of travel to compensate for the sloshing of the coffee, which has been at rest and would like to stay that way. But by the time the cruise is set at 79 (86 if Sims is driving), the coffee has acclimated to the motion and the cup can be held level. Which means the formula that would describe this cup-tipping isn't governed by speed, but by acceleration, the first derivative. My calculus is rusty at best, but I remember the notation as lovely. The symbol for integral, slender and curving, looks like one of the f-holes on a violin.

A day on the road as a touring musician promises ninety minutes of bright lights and twenty-two and a half hours of transit, setup, teardown, and restless sleeps in shared beds.

Tour makes my brain jumpy; like a pet that hasn't been walked, I get overeager for exercise and conversation. When a pair of primatologists came to my last show in Berlin, I begged them to stay afterward to talk awhile. I got too drunk to remember all the details, but we stayed a long time at the merch booth and they humored me with a little free lecture. They said chimps live in unit groups of forty to sixty. Some chimps crack nuts against stones, while some crack nuts against tree roots—unit groups just teach their young to do stuff differently. Those differences, the researchers said, might be considered essentially *cultural*. I leaned in and said, "Oooh, that's a controversial idea, right?" Depends on who you're talking to, they answered. Zoo primatologists never use *culture*—"the C-word"—but the field guys are more open to the idea. I thought the zoo team sounded greedy and stuck-up, trying to keep culture, morals, and tools for human use alone. Then again, I was exhausted and drinking whiskey and oversensitive.

On European tours, like the one I'm on now, we often travel by rail. Last night's show was in Manchester, England—a private party in a fancy hotel. My friend and DJ, Paper Tiger, performed with me. Now we're on board a train headed to tonight's gig in Bristol, where we'll reunite with the rest of the Doomtree guys. We're seated as far away from each other as two passengers could be: Paper's seat is in the last car, F, and I'm in A, a whole report card away. We're now stopped in the woods and the train hasn't moved for over an hour. Because it's just killed someone.

When we first stopped, a woman came down the aisle to speak to each of us individually. I heard her tell the man in front of me: *We've been involved in an incident. We don't yet know how long we'll be delayed.* Then she came to me and I leaned toward her to receive the message like a communion wafer.

When the delay stretched past twenty minutes, the catering cart started giving out free sandwiches in my car. I asked for a second sandwich and walked it back to Paper. He asked if I heard anything when it happened. Papes (most everyone in Doomtree goes by three names—we're like a Russian novel) wears Ray-Bans and pressed shirts, buttoned all the way up. I told him it happened in two parts: the small thud of the initial impact and then, as we were passing over the body, the sound diminished with each successive set of wheels.

By the time the formal announcement came over the PA, I had returned to my own seat. *Obviously, we've been in an incident,* a woman's voice began. A long time passed before she continued. She explained that we had to wait for emergency personnel to come and meet us in the woods. Her voice gave out at the end of every phrase, like a top wobbling off axis. I wondered where this woman was located on the train. Probably in a little closety office with a black handset on the wall, like a phone booth. I imagined her trembling between phrases, capable of mustering the dispassionate tone that must be used when speaking into the phone for only a few seconds at a time. Somewhere an org chart with roles and responsibilities probably determined which employee is supposed to make this sort of announcement—most likely the lead attendant. But listening to her struggle, it seemed that this duty would have been better assigned to whomever on board knew and liked the driver the least—whomever would be least affected by him holding his head in his hands in his cockpit, waiting for a doctor to arrive and tell him what he already knew. And what he must now tell his wife.

Now the train attendants apologize every quarter hour. They are very appreciative of our patience. People call their secretaries/boyfriends/nannies to inform them that they will be missing the meeting/can just hail a cab/should not be expected at dinner. I text Becky, who advances my tours, to let her know that Paper and I might not make the sound check in Bristol. And that it feels awful to be on this train. I don't like all the apologizing—very civil, sterile, very strange.

A woman seated nearby says she has a friend who works in trains. She says that after this sort of thing, drivers get a whole week off, and that they go straight to counseling. A week seems so obviously, grossly insufficient that I wonder if I am naïve in my understanding of the nature of this incident (which feels like an unduly delicate way of avoiding the word *accident*). Maybe it happens all the time. Maybe the driver had a week off just last year, maybe there is some drivers' slang for these extra vacation days, maybe he has memorized the psychiatrist's questionnaire, which must be administered—*letter of the law, buddy, bear with me*—to ensure that he has not been traumatized. Maybe there is a code in the inventory spreadsheet to track how many "incident sandwiches" were comped by the catering cart. Maybe the expense of these sandwiches is built into the price of all the train tickets.

I've heard that it's impossible for a train engineer to avoid hitting a person on the tracks ahead. Factoring in the human response time, the momentum, the friction brakes—by the time a human form is near enough to be perceived, it's already too late and the train can't be stopped in time. Last night, I would have confidently related that fact at a bar, but now I'm not sure where I heard it or if the source was credible.

Men in blaze orange vests arrive to the site. I can see them outside through the windows, taking photos of what happened. They walk the length of the train. One of them stops right outside my window and aims his large camera somewhere below my seat. If I could calculate the angle just right, I could position myself to catch the scene reflected in his dark lens. A pool shark would know just where to stand to bounce the image off the glass. I stay seated.

I have been preoccupied with death—mine and other people's—since I was a kid. I consider myself the steward of the old woman I will become, and I'm aware that with every day, we are closer to the same person. My parents used to joke that I was eight going on forty: I was a middle-aged baby boomer trapped in a little girl's body, worrying about money, and aging, and the brevity of this entire human experience. I've always been keenly and uncomfortably aware that all of my ambitions have a deadline; I have to get all this stuff done before my body fails. It's part of the reason I get restless on tour: *these hours are numbered, I can't afford to waste any in transit.*

The woman comes on the intercom again. We've been given the official all clear. *We thank you again for your patience and understanding.* Pause. *Today's total delay: ninety-four minutes.* There is only one more station before Bristol, where Paper and I will disembark. I decide to do a little math.

Given that a southbound train is delayed by ninety-four minutes, how many people would have to be on board for the sum total of their delays to equal the length of one human lifetime?

Let d equal the length of the delay: 94 minutes.

Any span of time can now be expressed in terms of d. A day, for example, is just over 15 delays long, or $15d$. A year is $5,591d$.

A person of unknown race and gender living in England has a life expectancy of 79 years.

Let l equal 79 years: 1 life.

The initial question—how many delays are equivalent to a lifetime—can be notated: $xd=l$.

To solve for x, I have to convert those 79 years into minutes and then divide that figure by 94. I pull up the calculator app on my phone and figure that $441,727d = l$. One life can be expressed as the combined inconvenience of 441,727 people delayed for 94 minutes.

How long would the train be that could accommodate 441,727—nearly half a million passengers?

I email a few questions to Becky. She's a crackerjack researcher—used to be a librarian. Within minutes, she replies with answers, citing her sources. Each train car is about 24 meters long, including the gangways. The capacity of each car averages 52 passengers. Becky also sends me a link to a news story about the accident, now picked up by the press. I skim it, looking for information about the person dead beneath my seat, but there are no details. I go back to the math.

The train that could hold half a million riders would be 127 miles long. It would have 8,494 cars. That's the minimum length of a train that could warrant all this apologizing, I think—where the loss on board begins to approach the loss below.

But a train of that length is unlikely to kill a man, because a train that long would barely have to move—it would almost span the distance of the whole journey from Manchester to Bristol. So to take the trip, one would simply walk south, stepping car to car. Each would house its own community, a discrete unit group of fifty-two, with its own rules of class and culture. Walking south, the dialects would change; the songs for birth and war and marriage would be transposed into new scales; the hot cars would go nearly naked, the cold ones cloaked in fur. And when she grew hungry, the traveler would kneel over her cache of nuts and make use of what was offered—tree root or stone—to take her meal. Or perhaps the traveler would be handed a sandwich wrapped in cellophane with which to mourn the dead.

Milk

The trick to formulating a good would-you-rather question is finding the fulcrum of pain. You've got to balance the question right there, on the point at which both alternatives seem equally unconscionable.

"Could you date someone who didn't believe in global warming? Or, wait, could you date a Holocaust denier? Like if they were perfect—the love of your life in every other way?" Sims, I think, asked that one. Sims does CrossFit and has blue eyes and insanely long eyelashes that bother him because they smash against the inside of his sunglasses. He's usually got a three-day beard and the cleanest clothes of anyone in Doom-tree. We joined the crew at the same time, quit smoking at the same time, and are both stubborn enough to occasionally butt heads on band business stuff. He's one of my favorite people.

The rest of us in the van, en route to Madison, contemplated his question. Would we rather abandon a once-in-a-lifetime romance or spend our lives loving unreasonable bigots?

Sims put a thumb on the scale. "And they're *vocal* about it, like, active on Internet forums and stuff."

We all groaned. Shit, I couldn't do it, I said. Even if I could stifle my conscience, I'd just be too embarrassed at parties.

We made it to Madison, loaded in the gear, and milled around the cold basement of the club, waiting to sound check. We ate corn chips and hummus, which is what all musicians everywhere eat before sound check. When the caveman carved the first bone flute from the femur of a deer, he ate a corn chip with hummus before playing the inaugural note.

I asked the group, "Would you rather be submerged in a bathtub full of kombucha, milk, or marinara sauce?"

"For how long?"

"Like, fifteen minutes, half an hour."

"Could I wear a condom?"

"Sure."

I thought this question might be a nonstarter—was already thinking of ways to modify it—but to my surprise a couple of the guys picked kombucha.

"Ew. Really?"

"Yeah," said Paper Tiger. He did a little shimmy. "Bubbles, man."

But milk is *clearly* the correct answer, I said. Cleopatra bathed in milk; the phrase "milk and honey" conveys luxury and decadence; lotion is practically just thick milk. It wasn't even a good question, because the answer was so obviously MILK.

X, who'd been long considering the alternatives, piped up with his answer: marinara.

At least one set of eyes rolled—some crew members suspected

that this was a purely contrarian maneuver. I wasn't so sure. In almost all dimensions, X is an unusual dude.

There was an outpouring of anti-marinara sentiment. It'd be impossible to rinse off. It's acidic. The only time people ever *willfully* submerge themselves in a tomato base—let alone a meaty sauce—is because they've been skunked. We waited to see if he'd reconsider.

X has a particular way of screwing up his face that wrinkles his nose; it's a charming, boyish expression. I think he knows it's a charming, boyish expression because sometimes he does it in press photos.

"I just think I'd like marinara."

Seven or eight years ago, X and I tried couples counseling— our second shot at it. We weren't even dating, we were just *thinking* about dating again and we set up the appointment as an exploratory mission. Maybe if we were more careful and deliberate than we'd been on previous attempts, this one would take.

For all the turmoil in our history, a strange calm always came over me when I knew for sure that X still loved me and that we might still have a chance together. It was like boarding a ship in rough weather, in wind and rain and lightning, but at the same time also feeling the undertow go still—the sensation that far below the surface something was settled. Maybe that's just the nature of strong love: it provides an elemental security, even if it jeopardizes almost everything else.

X arrived late to the counseling appointment. I was counting the minutes of this lateness so I could use them later as evidence of his noncommittal attitude, maybe even make a case for general unreliability depending on how long I sat alone. When he walked in, he apologized, then handed me a book titled *The Ethical Slut*.

The Ethical Slut is the *What to Expect When You're Expecting* of the polyamory scene. It's the go-to text for tactical advice on how to date more than one person at the same time. This gift was not on my wish list.

We were called to meet our counselor: a young, fair-skinned brunette with a good listening face. I alternated between contained hysteria, uncontained hysteria, and reasoned appeals that I directed exclusively at the counselor, who I considered the only other rational entity in the room. What in the holy fuck was he *thinking*? I struggled to keep my voice at a speaking volume, but managed to retain the weird formal tone that I revert to when I'm cornered—some animals, when threatened, squirt ink or break off their own tails; I go into a blend of Siri and Nathaniel Hawthorne.

X, I explained, had been unfaithful during our first relationship. And we're just barely starting to *entertain* the *possibility* of restoring that broken bond of trust. And the first thing he does is hand me a book about sleeping with other people. She gently reminded me that this meeting was just an informational consultation.

X and I didn't schedule a follow-up appointment. It was a long time before we considered getting back together again.

Years later, though, I had friends who were polyamorous. They were successful, married friends with home loans and full dental. Although it was still unusual, it didn't seem like the bit of fringe insanity it had been at first. I discovered so many of my peers were privately poly, in fact, that I started to wonder if I was the last artsy kid to believe in pair bonding. I felt like a stork, blinking stupidly beneath the brim of her cap at a party full of Playboy bunnies.

I read a few chapters of *The Ethical Slut*. I didn't like it. The metered, condescending tone of self-help books grates on me. The introduction implied that I was a square about to be freaked out for her own good. On a site called Reddit, however, I came across what felt like a very different conversation about polyamory between the musician Amanda Palmer and her writer husband, Neil Gaiman. They had an open relationship and they discussed it frankly, answering questions from their fans.

I am intrigued and impressed and a little intimidated by Amanda Palmer. I don't know her well, but I got to open for her once, at a stop on her book tour. Backstage I mentioned that I was planning to travel to New York and she arranged for me to stay in her Manhattan apartment for a few days. She didn't ask for references or a security deposit. She didn't even ask for my last name. And I thought to myself, *I want to be more like that, to take the risk on kindness. Sure, you'll get burned sometimes, but think of all the life you miss by playing it safe.*

Online, when fans asked about the mechanics of the relationship between Amanda and Neil, he responded: "It works okay currently because we have people we can kiss all over the world. If we both lived in a small town and never left, we might decide it was easier to have a closed relationship. Or we might not. . . . We talk. And talk. And talk. And hug a lot. And talk some more. And then do whatever needs to be done in the real world."

That all sounded so reasonable and compassionate—not at all like the powder-headed love junkies in my imagination. Was this sort of polyamory something I could or should consider if it might allow me to have a lasting relationship with *X*? It seemed like either the most pathetic, or the most woke, course of action a woman could entertain. *Alright, use your brain,* I thought. I took inventory: I had five big reservations about polyamory. I wrote them down and then tried to counter each one.

1. My gut says monogamy has moral virtue—that's just how love is best done.

Well, guts say a lot of things. And throughout the course of human history, guts have been epically, disastrously wrong. Particularly when they're aligned with prevalent cultural attitudes that have outlasted their utility.

Maybe this monogamy thing is just the vestige of a medieval Judeo-Christian moral code, more concerned with property rights than romantic intimacy. Even if monogamy was somehow "natural" to us, that still wouldn't make it morally right. Among a lot of primates, cannibalism is natural too.

2. If my dude loved someone else, there'd be less left
    for me.

If love were a Snickers bar, this would be true. But when a mother has a second child, we don't presume that she can only love her first kid half as much. It's not necessarily a zero-sum game; love wells up new when you meet someone who's precious to you.

However, I love milk chocolate and salmon *nigiri*. But I can't love them very well at the same time. Also, everybody who's rebounded with a fling knows how well new love can spackle over the old.

3. Polyamory is terrifying.

What if he meets someone he likes more and leaves me for her?

Totally possible. But if a partner genuinely stands a better chance at a real, lasting happiness with someone else, wouldn't the *loving* thing be to let them go? Polyamory or not, the idea of chasing smart, funny, attractive women out of the yard—lest they make my guy happy—sounds like a lousy way to live.

4. Being someone's sole romantic partner makes me
    feel special.

That's true. But also lame—why should my happiness hinge on feelings my partner *doesn't* have?

On the other hand, maybe monogamy is just a baked-in, inherited preference. Like, hello, I have brown eyes and type O blood and I want to form a life bond with only one dude who wants a life bond with only one me.

On the other, other hand, maybe it's just one of many possible learned modes of expression, like English. If so, is it something that I could unlearn for a fuller experience? It's hard to tell what's native and what's socialized—like trying to taste your own tongue.

5. I am totally unwilling to define *polyamory* to my dad at Thanksgiving.

I'm entirely too square to go around telling people I'm sleeping with a bunch of dudes at the same time. A lot of people are privately poly, but I don't have the wherewithal for a double life. And although I admire the zero-fucks-given attitude of my radical friends, I give plenty of fucks. I hand them out like perfume samples at the mall, in fact. I care what my family thinks, what colleagues think, what passing strangers and the children in their strollers think.

Telling my parents that I was seeing more than one guy would be excruciatingly uncomfortable. And it would be almost unimaginable to explain that my boyfriend was seeing other women. I can picture my father's face, hurt by and for me, questions sinking through him like arrows fired from all directions.

My family members have undermined the institution of marriage through the conventional channels—separation and divorce. Although both of my parents are unusual people, they have pretty traditional family values. My dad says that when he was a little boy he had two big dreams: he wanted to fly airplanes and get married. Dad won on both counts: he's now an accomplished glider pilot and married to a very smart woman named Leslie. He'd been married twice before, however: first to my mother and then to Linda, a lady I still consider family although we don't have a word for our relationship. (Introducing someone as *my ex-stepmother* sounds about as intimate as *my dentist-in-law*.) The experience of divorce not only broke my dad's heart, but, I think, rattled the foundations of his self-concept. Being gentlemanly and loyal is enormously important to him—if my dad likes an actress or singer on TV, the raciest thing he's likely to say is, "She's got class." A few times a year he finds reason to proudly announce, "I'm a one-woman man" to whoever's in the living room. His brand of moralism doesn't involve too many shades of grey. My brother and I have both inherited this system of thinking; I overpay my taxes every year, terrified of taking an unearned deduction.

My mom, meanwhile, has become very religious since her remarriage to David, a chiropractor with whom she lives in rural Wisconsin. If she were to run across a flock of sluts, it's unlikely she'd be interested in sorting them into ethical and unethical varietals.

My five-point list served to clarify my intellectual position on polyamory, but was it worth trying with *X*? I still wasn't sure.

Chuck Klosterman is a good formulator of would-you-rathers. He wrote a deck of them called HYPERtheticals that kept

Doomtree occupied between the load-ins and the hangovers of a trip to South by Southwest. One of the cards asked whether or not readers would attempt to kick a healthy, but immobilized, Clydesdale to death, if success would trigger the release of every political prisoner on earth. The kicker would be permitted steel-toe boots and twenty minutes to get the job done. My crewmate Mike Mictlan and I sat on opposite benches in the tour bus and opposite sides of the issue. Mike has impeccable dramatic timing, a tattoo on his left temple, and a sweet tooth to rival mine—a rarity. He waxed eloquently about moral obligation, hope, and duty. I drunkenly image searched *Budweiser Horse*, unable to spell *Clydesdale*, but confident Mike couldn't possibly realize how big the motherfuckers were.

Undiscouraged by the picture of the beast I showed him, Mike held firm. He insisted that with so much at stake, you have to try—you just have to try.

High stakes and long odds make for especially unpleasant deliberation. If I remember correctly, something like four thousand bands performed at South by Southwest that year. We all pressed together on Sixth Street in Austin, Texas, wearing the same black jeans and combat boots, trying to find the loading door or the free booze or a missing guitarist. SXSW can feel like a festival of lines—people waiting to get into the secret show, the best taco place, the bathroom. Promotional teams on every corner hand out sunglasses, flyers, energy drinks. And all of us thousands of musicians hope to somehow rise above the din, to impress the right reporter or shake the right hand that could warrant this incredible spend of time and money. (Modest hotel rooms can be five hundred dollars a night during the festival. All seven members of Doomtree once slept in a rented camper van parked on an incline.) Every year there are a few bands who manage to win SXSW; they emerge as buzzy media darlings with enough magic on them to really catalyze a career.

All of us understood the chances were slim; we'd probably just return home sunburnt, spent, and in the red. But most years, we still go to Austin. To kick the damn horse.

A couple of summers ago, X and I took a walk through a downtown park, having one of our should-we-give-this-another-go conversations. With the city rising on all sides, we took laps around the manicured trails on a tiny hike through the little simulated wilderness.

He hadn't been in a monogamous relationship for years, but it was something he'd be willing to consider with me, he said. He asked gentle questions to see how I really felt about the prospect of polyamory. *Think of your trip to Turkey*, he said. I'd recently returned from Istanbul, where I'd traveled with my best friend, Jaclyn, for a while, then gone solo to try to sort out my head. *If you wanted to, you could make out with someone while you're there—and I would know that doesn't affect how you feel about me.* We could design it so that we only dated people who lived in different cities—maybe those secondary relationships wouldn't even involve intercourse. There were no rules, he said. We could invent anything we wanted together.

Even though I could imagine female friends rolling their eyes (*Of course men want to have sex with every woman they meet, all the time!*), I knew this conversation wasn't just about sex. X was a charming, talented rapper—he could have all the sex he wanted without all these gutting conversations and teary good-byes with me. He was a man who'd struggled with standard models of intimacy, and he learned about an unconventional way of living that felt well suited to him. And he was trying to decide how much he was willing to give up to be with a woman he loved, but feared hurting, having done so before.

I told X that I'd started to wonder if polyamory might be an orientation, not a lifestyle. When I first had that idea, it kicked back like a shotgun I hadn't known I was holding. Trying to change someone's *orientation* was unthinkable—only closeted evangelists did that. And it never worked anyway.

So, if I were a native monogamist and he weren't, would it even be hypothetically possible for people of different orientations to mate for life?

Would you rather have a spectacular love with an unusual man and share him with other people or wait for an ordinary love that you got to keep all to yourself?

People change religions for one another; they renounce citizenships, adopt children, they lose weight, take new names.

Almost anything about a person can change.

For 5K there's a company that will laser the brown out of your eyes, revealing the blue iris beneath.

The blood type of a little girl with rubella changed from A to O.

Meadow voles are naturally promiscuous, but if you juice

46

up their little vole brains with high levels of a protein called the vasopressin receptor, they'll begin to behave like prairie voles—monogamists that pair for life.

But even presuming I *could* go poly, was I even allowed to make a compromise of that magnitude for a man? Which feminist street gang would jump me for my membership card first: the one that's mad I conceded so much for a man or the one that's mad I'm not sex-positive enough to be out there balling other dudes already?

Walking through the park, *X* and I made compelling cases on both sides of the argument for reconciliation. If we failed, we might lose our friendship—and subject ourselves to even more pain. But the stakes seemed too high not to try—think of all we'd miss by playing it safe.

No matter how we maneuvered the question, the scales held perfectly level. It was impossible to decide. We punted. We wouldn't try now, but in the future—maybe.

Maybe when we're forty, he said. Maybe he'll like white wine by then, and we'll live together, and we'll have sorted all this out. Part of me wanted him to insist we just jump in headlong. But no part of me was willing to instigate that sort of headlong jumping myself. We left the park, had a sad hug, and walked to our stupid cars.

Camped out on our fulcrum, we lived undecided for a long time.

At family holidays, when my dad and his brothers are running down the Greatest Hits of their boyhood anecdotes, I often request somebody tell the one about the salamander and the milk.

When my dad was a boy, he caught a salamander. He took it home and set it up in a little terrarium with leaves and twigs to simulate the whole of nature. He promptly fell in love with it in the way kids love to play house with wild things. That night, when his mother served dinner for him and his brothers, he pushed away from the table and ran to the terrarium. *What about Sal? I bet he's hungry too!* He went to the refrigerator to find something to serve for dinner. He pulled a carton out of the fridge, then went back to the salamander's cage and gently picked him up by the hinge of his jaw. The salamander hung like a test tube: body slack, mouth open.

My dad was so sure of the answer that he hadn't realized there was a question. With a steady hand, total concentration, and the blunt tool of his own tenderness, he carefully filled his salamander with milk. He then took his place at the table, smiling and self-satisfied. Because that is how love is done.

Lights from Above

At takeoff I can feel my organs press backward. I shut my paperback, freezing its assorted characters mid-dilemma. Soon the pockets of air in my sinuses will bloom in my head, and the nail polish in my carry-on will begin to seep, perfuming my underthings with acetate. The Wi-Fi icon will turn on and the signal will pass through all of us, searching for antennae in our purses and our pockets. The seatbelt light will turn off, and some of us in coach will head toward the back lavatory, shuffling through the aisle at approximately 2 miles an hour, which brings the forward rate of travel down to 598 miles per hour. There is an armed plainclothes air marshal on board to keep the peace. Or maybe he is on the flight behind us.

Usually the shadow of a plane grows larger and fainter as it ascends. But planes in flight can also create something like the opposite of a shadow—when sunlight refracts around the fuselage just so, it focuses into a bright spot below. My dad has explained the science to me several times, but I can never quite remember how it works. Still, whenever I've got a window seat, I try to look for it: a bright spot tracking over fields below. I don't know if these beams of light can be seen by people on the ground—I've never felt one pass over: a spotlight sweeping across the highway, or a surge of white light bursting through the kitchen window.

On this trip, I did score a window seat and I can see my reflection in the scratched plastic pane. My new china doll haircut looks like a wig—like I'm a poorly protected witness or a cartoon spy. Sometimes people ask if my hair is real or if what was my signature braid is somehow tucked beneath it. When I get offstage after a concert, flushed and sweating, sometimes a fan will try to pull to check.

Over the PA, a regal baritone voice informs us that we are in a holding pattern over JFK. We are not allowed to land, but we are not supposed to leave. Idle circles, like a woman's finger on a wineglass in a second-rate seduction scene.

I have come to New York because back in Minneapolis I have been asked to write an opera—a thing that I have no idea how to do. I'm a rapper and a pop vocalist; my first association with *Carmen* would be *Sandiego*. But when the director approached me, I said yes because he seemed smart and I was flattered. Also, I was afraid to say no; I'm mid-career now and miles away from where I hoped I'd be. I'd imagined that by the time I hit my thirties, I'd have paid my dues on the club circuit and upgraded from a rattling passenger van to a tour bus. I'd have a home somewhere and in it I'd have a dining set with matching chairs. I imagined laughing during interviews about the days of piling five musicians into one hotel room or hiding hard-boiled eggs in paper coffee cups to smuggle them out of the continental breakfast room and into the van for lunch. But I'm still playing the same clubs every year, still foraging at the breakfast bar. At this point, I'll jump at most opportunities to write or perform for a big audience. So I made a Spotify playlist of famous operas to get to work. And I found myself wishing there were more choruses.

I asked if I could cast the production with pop singers. The director said I could have a few, but would need opera voices too. I asked if I could stage it in a warehouse or something. He said go to New York. See *Sleep No More*. Then we'll talk again.

I've rarely spent so much on a ticket for anything, except for maybe the open-bottle ticket I got on tour for a forgotten bottle of whiskey in my backpack. The production had been sold out for months. The website said I'd have to wear a mask for the whole show.

Circling over JFK, I offer the nervous white-haired woman beside me a piece of gum. Gum is the remedy for every malady of air travel—pressure in the ears, restlessness, boredom, fear. Like the leeches of medieval physicians, Doublemint does everything.

We are cleared to approach and touchdown is gentle. I go to Midtown and check into Pod 51, a hotel with impossibly tiny, modular rooms. The square footage allows for one twin bed, a desk exactly the dimensions of an open book, and a strip of carpet wide enough for sit-ups. I do a set of twenty. There's a sink the size of a soup bowl and an aluminum hook that folds out of the wall to hang a jacket. It's like living in a pop-up book. Lights above the door conveniently indicate which of the bathrooms on Floor 4 are occupied and which are vacant.

When I'm not touring with Doomtree, I usually travel by myself. It can be lonesome: there's no one to split lunch with, no one to help with the schlepping or the navigation, no one with whom to marvel at the sites or commiserate after the pickpocketing. But traveling alone also makes a person fully available—to chat with the bartender and maybe go to the after-hours hang, or make faces at little kids on the bus, to arrive at your own assessments of the street food or the museum piece without the influence of someone else's commentary. You can scrap plans, or wedge into a full tram, or have another drink, or say nothing at all for hours, without consulting or offending or boring anyone. On the occasions that I feel blue on the road, I'll often tell myself *Loneliness is the fare that you pay to be free.* Visiting New York to see *Sleep No More*, however, felt like a great adventure. The sense of purpose squared my shoulders and lifted my chin. *Purposeful* might be my favorite feeling—even better than happiness.

One of your artsy friends has probably seen *Sleep No More*, or maybe you have seen it and you are the artsy friend. It's an adaptation of *Macbeth* that's been running for years in an old hotel. There's no stage; the characters rove freely through the floors, and audience members follow whomever they please. Couples are encouraged to split up. No speaking allowed.

Macbeth arouses a lot of superstitions among actors. Some think the spells written into the dialogue are real, that they summon evil spirits into theaters. A string of performers, stagehands, and audience members have died during perfor-mances. (The onstage combat scenes provide ample opportu-nities for injuries.) Many performers won't even say *Macbeth* aloud in a theater before the show starts—bad luck. Instead, the production is referred to simply as "the Scottish play."

The night of the performance is brutally cold. Navigating on my phone, I fast-walk from the subway with my head down. At the specified address, there's no sign, just a tall door and a single overhead light. When I come near, however, a long-haired white woman with a clipboard approaches, asks what I'm looking for and then says, "If you'll just show your ID, we'll get you inside." She looks away from me and the door swings open. Inside, I join a long, quiet line of people. The orderly hush makes it feel like we're on the jetway to a play.

After tickets are taken, we're all routed into in an old-world barroom: red velvet curtains on the walls, a little stage with a silver bullet mic, and tiny cocktail tables—really just coasters on stems. The bar staff is outfitted in speakeasy attire with vests and armbands like newsies. *Okay, fine*, I think. There's a familiar smell: the airborne sweetness of chemical haze, which smells a little bit like what I remember paste tasting like in preschool. I order a beer and elbow through the chattering crowd to take a seat at one of the little tables. A newsie finds me—I'd forgotten my credit card at the bar like an amateur. He returns my Mastercard, flipping it at me with a flourish as if he'd pulled it from my ear.

A camera flash goes off and the nearest waiter lunges, like a fencer, to slice his drink tray down over the offender's iPhone as an enormous lens cap. They are serious about the no-photo policy. The room fills to capacity.

I am aware of sitting alone in a room full of couples.

What a dress, says a female voice beside me. A blonde with Monroe curls and matte red lips has taken stage. She wears a flesh-colored slip with vertical black stripes and a deep V that precludes the possibility of a bra. She is illegally beautiful. She leans over slowly, bringing her red lips to the silver microphone.

I reach into my pocket and pull out a Pod 51 ballpoint pen, ready to take notes. Monroe sees me. I know she's now likely to assume I am a critic. It's funny how a stolen hotel pen and some scratch paper can tip the seesaw of power, sliding it from a showstopping blonde in a lethal dress to a woman in a charcoal sweater who cut her own bangs before leaving her rented room.

In small groups, the blonde calls us into a corner of the room. She hands me a white mask, fluted at the bottom like a beak. When I fasten it behind my head, it amplifies the sound of my breathing.

I'm ushered into an elevator with a dozen other attendees. We ascend one story standing like a phalanx of storks, white faces deadpan and identical. The door opens to a dimly lit hallway and we're free to go as we please. I wait for my eyes to adjust. Somewhere to my left there's the sound of a scuffle. Barefoot and crazy-eyed, a woman storms past me—Lady Macbeth. I follow her at a jog, along with the rest of the flock. Lady Macbeth, when she's not Lady Macbething, is clearly a trained dancer, her muscles are like tree roots grown over the trellis of her skeleton. I skim the plotline of the play in my head, wondering what scene I could be running into. If memory serves, at the beginning of the play she should have an exchange with her husband, who she'll scold for his cowardice.

But then I break away from her and trail a pair of fighting men whose roles I can't recall. Who *are* these dudes? They're very fit—in their duel they tumble over each other and sometimes up the walls. It occurs to me that in a traditional production, these characters might not make an entrance so early in the play. But here at the hotel, it seems every performer plays his or her role all evening, with no sense of being on- or off-stage. That's how our real lives unfold, I think. It's impossible to know which moments are crucial to your narrative until the story is over. The character you now know as the leading man might, in the final draft, be referred to only as The First Husband. That week of stomach flu is actually morning sickness— a minor subplot, because you never find out you're pregnant and miscarry only three days later. The opera funding will fall through in the next round of budget cuts and you will be back playing nightly gigs in midsize venues, struggling to pull the sail of your ambition up the mast of your career.

At the end of the performance, audience members wind up in the same barroom. We remove our masks, shake out our hair. The crowd churns as separated dates recouple, eager to compare their evenings. Pushing through the heavy door, I head into the wind, hood pulled low.

I feel sorry, in a way, for all the minor characters who worked so hard all night. Each one would perceive himself as the axis of the action. For the sitting king, the play isn't called *Macbeth*, it's called *Duncan*. For the heir it's *Malcolm*; and for The Porter it's, well, it's whatever his name is, which wasn't even dignified with a mention in the script.

But a play can't have a dozen leads; there aren't enough spotlights. And there's a story arc—the profile of a church bell—that must be adhered to. In *Macbeth*, there's a prophecy to fulfill. Those old plays always have the decency to subvert their characters with fate. And fate at least knows what it's doing; there's some semblance of a plan. Even if you're mowed over in the execution of it. In life we are more often matched against chance and circumstance: blind, mole-like circumstance, burrowing dumb and mute and unaware that we exist at all.

Life is strewn with landmines that can blow you out of your own story. I've slept with three moderately famous men: a musician, a photographer, and a military figure. I admired each of them, and was admired back. But I recognized the implicit danger: with famous men, one risks being cast as a Zelda. The first man used to tap my thigh in bed, fretting the chords to what would become a song on the radio. The second took my photo half-dressed in a hotel room, then developed it in the bathroom in a tumbler full of silver nitrate. The third is retired from combat, mulling over a bid for political office. And if their trajectories go skyward, I'll be rendered a footnote in their biographies.

Even if you dodge all the landmines and retain the starring role, you might find yourself in a story that wouldn't interest you. That's why I don't buy lottery tickets: I'd hate to win. A million-dollar jackpot would pivot my whole narrative on five random numbers—that would be the biggest story of me, the one I'd be asked to tell at cocktail parties with my new rich friends and it'd be one that would strain all my phone calls with my old poor friends too. A story signifying nothing.

· My concern isn't about legacy, exactly. That's an old man's game. It's more about agency, about trying to minimize the role of chance and maximize the role of will. If you can't parse the merit from the luck, it's hard to know what to think of yourself.

I arrive at my hotel room: a prop closet with just enough room to stow my sleeping body. I set my mask on the narrow ledge at the foot of the bed. I shut my eyes. Overhead, tiny lights blink on and off as other hotel guests shuffle to and from the lavatories.

In real time, you go through life like an actor from whom her role has been kept secret. Is my character a hard-touring pop singer with a crooked smile? Could she be one break away from something bigger? Or maybe she is only the nameless half-dressed model in a portrait, posed in a hotel room to re-create an Edward Hopper painting she had never seen? You never feel the spotlight sweeping over; it's impossible to know when you're on stage and when you're off. Maybe I have no speaking lines at all. Maybe I am only crossing through someone else's drama and a name I've never heard will be rendered in the italics of the title role, letters falling forward toward the future, the eastern margin of the page.

A Ringing in the Ears

When my dad looks through his telescope he says, *Hello, Jupe*, on a first-name basis with every moon and planet. He's learned Morse code, Latin, and Irish jigs arranged for accordion. He's interested in almost everything but money—left Mensa after deeming it a confederacy of snobs who met to congratulate one another on cheating people at their own garage sales. He talks to himself, in full voice and often in third person, while executing any multistep task. When he was in his thirties, my age now, he was lean and dark haired, preoccupied and tired. Almost every waking moment of his life was accounted for: during the day he struggled as a trader on the grain exchange; most evenings he cooked dinner for me and my little brother, Maxie; at night he studied to earn a degree in audiology. And every spare, interstitial moment he devoted to his passion project in the dim confines of our garage. There he was building the Woodstock—a real airplane that he intended to fly.

Gliders are motorless aircraft. They ride thermals—invisible columns of rising warm air—to stay aloft. They're silent and sleek and they sail around like stingrays in the sky. The Wood-stock is a single-seater; the lone pilot tucks himself inside it, half-reclined, the stick between his knees. My dad's model had a thirty-nine-foot wingspan and weighed about 250 pounds. He started building the plane just before I was born. He esti-mated that it would take a year and a half to complete.

The engineers who designed the Woodstock sold prefab kits to be assembled by dedicated amateurs like my dad. How-ever, by the time he'd set his sights on making one, the kits were all gone. The designers had some paper plans left in stock, but building a plane from those would require cutting every wooden part by hand. It'd be like stopping at the grocery store for hamburger patties and receiving, instead, a live calf to raise to maturity for slaughter next season. He cut the check for a hundred and fifty bucks and bought the plans anyway.

He was still working on the plane when I started grade school. One had to tread carefully with Dad during the Wood-stock years: he had a hair-trigger temper and a particular sen-sitivity to interruptions. But his good side was great if you could make your way onto it. I was a precocious stick figure of a kid then, gap-toothed, hungry for praise, and just starting to exhibit some benign neuroses, on course for the high-strung adult I'd become: step counting, symmetrical touching, later a brief infatuation with prime numbers. Childhood never suited me very well; when my parents' friends came over, I ate the raw garlic spread and asked for sips from my dad's tumbler to demonstrate my refinement. I laughed at their jokes and used big words and considered myself unjustly exiled from the adult world on the trifling, circumstantial pretense that I was seven.

When my dad made his irreversible decision to build a wooden plane, he owned only a hacksaw, pliers, and possibly a pair of socket wrenches. His most recent carpentry project was the Popsicle stick box he'd glued together when he was twelve. He had never made a square cut through any piece of wood unassisted.

When I asked him many years later why he went ahead with it after finding out the kits were unavailable, he told me, "The only way I would ever get my hands on a new aircraft would be to build it myself. There was no chance whatsoever I would ever earn enough money to buy a new aircraft made by a factory." Fine, I thought, my dad never had a lucrative career path—before studying audiology, he'd earned his living performing and transcribing Elizabethan lute music—but why not just build a different glider? Why did it have to be the Woodstock? My dad's voice dropped a register. "I had *made the decision* that I was going to build this aircraft." My father can do many things that most people cannot—maritime navigation, an entertaining PowerPoint, a decent rendition of the Japanese song "Sakura Sakura" on a small medieval instrument called a psaltery—but it's as though he gained these unusual powers by relinquishing the ability to do some things that almost everyone else *can* do. My dad, like kangaroos and emus, cannot go backward.

A certain strain of absolutism runs through the whole side of my father's family. They—we—still use phrases like *man of his word* and compliment people by calling them *the genuine article*. Part of it, I think, is attributable to my grandfather's time in the navy. He enlisted young and served as a ranking officer on a destroyer. Duty and integrity loomed large in his world-view and in his household. All of his surviving sons inherited his values, my dad especially. When I was little, even small changes of plans—eating dinner at eight instead of seven—could take on a moral dimension. *We* said *the stir-fry would be served at seven P.M. central time and we* will *uphold that pledge.* Once he'd committed to the idea, building the Woodstock became a matter of honor.

To obtain the necessary raw materials, my dad introduced himself to the night watchman at a wholesale lumberyard in Saint Paul. After a small bribe changed hands, he was allowed to handpick the four finest boards from their inventory. He inspected thousands before selecting those that would become the wings of his airplane.

He hauled these old-growth boards to Roosevelt High School and enrolled in an eight-week community education class. Most of the other students were retirees. When the instructor asked what sorts of projects they planned to build, they answered, *A birdfeeder* or, *A jewelry box.* "And, Mr. Wander, what are *you* making?" Over the heads of his classmates and their shoeboxes full of birch chips, my dad answered, "I'm building an aircraft." He'd brought several hundred pounds of high-grade lumber balanced on a handcart, some of it twenty feet long.

His first task was actually to build the long table on which the other building could be done. Then he used the shop's machinery to mill and cut and plane the hundreds of parts he needed. At the end of the course, he mounted the freshly shaped wing spars on the roof rack of his station wagon and brought everything home to the garage for assembly.

My dad cussed, sanded, drilled, and mitered for the better part of a decade. He mixed amber-colored epoxy in beakers and spilled a considerable mess of it on the sidewalk, just outside the doorway of the garage. I thought of the resultant glossy puddle as a four-season ice rink.

It was nearly impossible to make one's self useful to him in the garage (particularly if one's self was only four feet tall and could not be trusted with a saw, vice, or epoxy blend). So, to impress my father, I memorized what I could of his audiology lessons instead. A plastic model of the inner ear sat on our dining room table, easy to study. Blown up to the size of a honeydew, the human auditory system looks more like something you'd find at the bottom of the ocean than inside your head. It's all cilia and tentacles and spiral bone chambers. I studied our centerpiece, learning the nautilus shape of the cochleae, the semicircular canals, and the tiny little bones that fit like clock parts, ready to recite them for my father.

His own studies were marked by exhaustion. He often fell asleep while reading after dinner; the right margins of his notebook pages were striped with arcing lines, where his writing hand had slid off the page as he nodded out. Sometimes he passed out on the living room carpet with ankles crossed and arms outstretched, like the shadow of an airliner.

I figured when he finally earned his degree and got his own office, I could work there as some sort of assistant. I was intrigued by deaf life: I loved the idea of being able to pick a sign for your own name, the idea of applauding a performance silently, with hands waving overhead. It seemed like a secret world embedded right inside the regular one—my first exposure to the idea of subculture. Years later I'd have a poster of the finger spelling alphabet on my bedroom wall and a prized hardcover called *The Joy of Signing*, an illustrated dictionary. Without anyone to practice with, I never really learned to read sign, but I did get halfway decent at translating pop songs on the radio—or at least I think I did and nobody was around to tell me otherwise. Interpreting for an imagined audience, I exaggerated my facial expressions and dancified the movements to convey the *feeling* of the music. It was like being both a figure skater and a telenovela starlet, with a reference book in her lap.

Sometimes my dad took me with him to the audiology lab. To be in a place where actual science happened felt phenomenally sophisticated. I even got to participate; during one visit, my father put me in a glass room and outfitted me with an oversized pair of headphones to serve as a research subject. The headphones made my head big and heavy, like a hatchling's. He told me to raise my hand whenever I heard a tone. The signals got quieter and quieter. I strained to detect them, excited to have a job and eager to dazzle with my keen hearing. My dad came in, looking stern. I was raising my hand when there were no tones. I was making false positives. I had to listen more carefully and only raise my hand when I was sure. I sat, waiting for the next round, ashamed to have failed him.

After my dad earned his degree, the plan was to move out

west and start a practice in Montana. While he studied, my mom did most of the breadwinning. She was a foxy New York Puerto Rican who'd come to the Midwest for the greenery and a career in broadcasting. Maxie wasn't quite two years old. He didn't show much interest in learning to talk, but conceded to use a few hand signs to further his own objectives. *More* was a house favorite. It's made by tapping the fingertips of both hands together, like two birds kissing. The four of us lived in a two-story house in residential Minneapolis, on the corner of Forty-Fourth Street and Forty-Fourth Avenue, an address I loved. My mother's used Camry was usually parked in front of the house because the garage was full of my father and his plane.

Two of the very last parts to be finished were the wings and the clear, curving canopy. The wing surface was to be made of fabric, wrapped taut around wooden spars, set with a heat gun, and brushed with several coats of butyrate aircraft dope. The canopy was supposed to be made of plexiglass.

Plexiglass, however, cracked easily. It resisted drilling. After destroying a hundred bucks' worth of the stuff, and working himself into a minor fury, my father adjusted course. "I decided that I needed to become a closer student of plexiglass, that I would risk only three or five dollars at a time until such time as I understood its characteristics." He started running some small-scale experiments in the microwave, trying to get the stuff to melt and drape over a mold as he intended. Very often the mold he used was one of my softballs. I'd be late for practice, trying to pry a plexiglass half shell off my gear before running to the park. Eventually, he abandoned the temperamental substrate altogether and bought a pane of more workable Lexan instead.

This was a particularly frustrating stage of construction for my father, during which it was best to keep a wide berth. The tare weight of a child's fear is not calibrated to an adult scale, so it's difficult now to know whether my response to his anger was proportionate, but I do know that I was very, very frightened by it. He shouted and swore when he was angry, went red-faced and moved with enough speed and force to flip his dark hair down over his forehead. When he came home, I sometimes zipped Maxie into a sleeping bag and tucked him into my closet for safekeeping until the coast was clear. (Years later, I discovered that a vein of the same anger ran through me; I was horrified to see Maxie looking on quietly as I nursed my hand after punching a wall.) My dad wasn't all temper during those years, though: he was also tender, poetic, and sentimental. When the Woodstock was nearly complete, he leaned inside the fuselage and wrote my name and Maxie's on the wing spars—where the heart would be, if a glider had one. Whatever else was volatile, his love was constant.

The day that my father opened the garage door to wheel his finished product into the alley, neighbors gathered to watch. Most had no idea what he'd been working on; the sounds of industry emanating from the Wander garage never seemed to result in any appreciable improvements to the house or yard. The door shuddered as my dad wrestled it up. He brought the plane parts out into the sunlight: the auburn wooden body, the

Lexan canopy shining like wet glass, and the pair of translucent fabric wings. With the help of a friend, he attached the wings to the body and there it was: *The Woodstock*. The physical forces that render sailplanes aerodynamic make them dramatic to look at—long and slender. My dad surveyed his work. Varnished wood is vivified by sunlight in much the same way that human hair is: strands of red and gold flame up for a moment and then resume their positions in the wood grain or the braid. In my giddiness I wanted to crowd him, but knew enough not to trample on the ceremony. Our neighbors' stupefied awe delighted me; to see their faces, my dad might have just walked a unicorn out of our garage.

By his count, the Woodstock took six years, eight months, fifteen days, and eight hours to complete. It cost three thousand dollars.

My father's attention could be hard to get for the same reasons it was worth getting—while other people's dads wore wide ties and coached soccer teams and went to work as account managers or sales representatives, my dad had turned himself into a kite. But there was only room for one in the Woodstock. And scarcity functions in human systems the way it does in all economies: it drives up value.

Over the next few years, my most familiar view of the Woodstock would be from below, sunlight glowing through the wings as it climbed out of sight. My dad said it was like flying a violin.

My parents' marriage started to give out soon after the plane was done. Their plans to move out west were canceled, which in turn canceled my dad's plan to start an audiology practice; the market in Minneapolis was already saturated. He didn't even bother showing up for the final exam—if he couldn't put it to proper use, a degree would be a waste of ink and frame and glass and paper. The details of my parents' conflicts, failed negotiations, and their respective heartbreaks are their own: not mine to tell, even if I knew the details of the story. I'm not sure exactly what my mother made of the plane. Maybe she was impressed by my father's skill and discipline. Maybe she was hurt by how much time he chose to spend alone in the garage. They weathered it out for another few years before making the final split.

No longer a prospective audiologist, my dad needed a professional Plan B. To buy himself some time, he decided to spend the summer as a glider flight instructor. He'd instructed before, but never with the idea that it might become a proper vocation. To his surprise, the phone rang off the hook—evidently a bunch of people wanted to learn to fly gliders. What he'd expected to be a three-month gig turned into a full-time career.

Maxie and I spent a lot of time at the airfield. It had grass runways and a fraying orange windsock and a vending machine in the hangar. We were usually the only kids there, and almost always I was the only female on the premises. Because gliders land silently, we had to be very, very careful. To avoid reprimand from an adult, we had to stage dramatic performances of carefulness, looking up, down, left, and right, like panic-stricken mimes—vigilant cowards tiptoeing through the grass.

The gliding community is not very big, but within it my dad became something of a celebrity. He earned a reputation as a first-rate pilot and an excellent teacher. He found thermals in novel places, riding the lift rising from mall parking lots, warmed by the asphalt and the engines of just-parked cars. Those thermals, he said, smelled like pizza. He wrote a book with a bright blue cover called *Learning to Fly Gliders* and sold it through the mail. The public television show *Newton's Apple* featured him in an episode called "Gliders/Suction Cups/ Novocain/Leeches." On screen, as in life, he looked like a handsomer Lou Reed and talked like an American Winston Churchill. He wrote more books during the off-season, lectured on a circuit, and put on a black suit to present and receive awards.

My dad used to tell his students, "You're not driving a bus with wings on it, you are flying like a bird, and if you cease flying like a bird, you will fall like a stone." He and his students flew alongside birds all the time; every soaring body relied on the same sources of lift. When the glider came near large birds of prey—pelicans, eagles, or vultures—my dad told his students, "Turn off the radio and make no speech sounds." Human noises would spook them, he said, but the aerodynamic sounds of aircraft—the wind streaming past, that wouldn't bother them at all. Both the birds and the glider pilots, he said, were accustomed to a soft, persistent rush.

To get airborne, the gliders were towed, usually by single-engine Piper Cubs or Cessnas. Most of the tow pilots were young; they were filling their logbooks with flight hours to qualify for a job with the commercial airlines. Sometimes I'd ride along on tow. After releasing the gliders, the tow pilots flew like daredevils, eager for any action. If you held a pen in your open hand while they dove back toward the runway, it would rise up and off your palm.

During my last summers at the airfield, I'd occasionally serve as wing runner. A glider's landing gear is a single wheel, so when it's on the ground one wing tip rests on the grass. To keep the craft level during takeoff, someone has to sprint along holding a wing steady—much like a parent holding the back of a bike seat on the first ride without training wheels.

As a teenager on the brink of real emotional trouble, I'd sometimes swipe my dad's flight jacket, to wear ironically over ripped tights and cutoffs. *Bob Wander's Soaring Books and Supplies | Ask me about soaring* was embroidered in arcing letters on the back. More than once I was stopped by a square-looking white guy wanting to know if I really was Wander's kid—if so, my old man was a hell of a pilot.

My father stands six foot even. I'm almost as tall, a writer and a touring musician now. I talk to myself, in full voice and often in third person, to execute any multistep task. Many of the factors that were stressors during my childhood are the strengths of our adult relationship. I've inherited his widow's peak, his curiosity, a share of his temper, and his work ethic. I stay up late researching my writing projects; I sleep with my phone beneath my pillow; I mutter half-written lyrics standing in line at the supermarket. When I visit my father's place looking fatigued, he doesn't harp on "work-life balance." If a song idea were to strike during Thanksgiving dinner, my dad would leave the table himself to make sure I had a pen and a private corner—and he'd run defense to ensure no well-intended family member interrupted with a plate of food. As adults we can share books and talk until midnight drinking iced martinis. And when he's caught in the updraft of some new enthusiasm—epigenetics or space flight—I can jog beside him, a wing runner.

My father is very proud of Maxie and me, and tells us as much. When I'm onstage, I can almost always tell where he's seated in the house. Even if it's a large room and the overhead lights are blinding, I'll hear his *Brava!* through the noise. For all the people hollering at a pop concert, there is only one likely to be doing so in gender-appropriate Italian.

Some dynamics, of course, do not change. My father was a fully formed person when he met me, whereas I imprinted on him. Waddling behind him, he shaped my ideas about the sort of creature I was supposed to become and I remain unduly influenced by his opinion. His thoughts about my music, for example, matter much more than would seem reasonable. I write and perform hip-hop songs; my dad is hardly a member of the target demographic. Still, when I recorded my first and second albums, I couldn't get him out of my head.

Would he like this part?

Which part—the part you're singing halfheartedly, distracted by this speculation?

Yes, that part.

Well, he's certainly not going to like that particular take. *Try again.*

I regularly find myself engaged in imaginary conversation with my father. I might be listening to NPR, say, when an author I admire stammers during an interview. And I'll hear my father's voice issue his oft-repeated mandate to public figures: *Speak like you write, sir!* I'll defend the author to my father: Not everybody's a natural orator, Pop. Before I know it, we're debating language and class while the radio blares on and I stand frozen at the kitchen sink, staring through the dishes.

Through my work in music, I received an invitation to visit an anechoic chamber: a room in Minneapolis that's supposed to be one of the quietest in the world. The floor, walls, and ceiling are covered in pyramids of brown foam. The visitor stands on a pane of wires, like a chain-link fence laid on its side. It's a small space, probably too small for a king-size bed. The entire concrete shell is mounted on a shock absorber to buffer it from any seismic rumbling. I'd read that the silence could be overwhelming; some people panicked inside the chamber, had auditory hallucinations. I was more concerned, however, with tinnitus—that I might discover a ringing in my ears that was obscured by the daily din of traffic and conversation. But I accepted the offer to spend a few minutes inside the chamber. When the door sealed shut, I sat down cross-legged on the chain-link floor. I sang a bit, but it sounded awful; with no echo at all, every vocal imperfection remained unnaturally crisp—like lunar craters with no wind to blow them smooth again. I could hear my respiration, the rush of blood, and the creaking of my joints as my heartbeat rocked me ever so slightly—the exertions of my organism keeping itself alive. There was no sustained high-frequency whine, as I'd feared, but I thought I heard a steady roar of white noise, which made me sad. That is the cost, I thought, of all these loud nights standing in front of snare drums and amplifiers. If you listen to anything long enough, you'll hear it forever.

Over the years, I've heard most of my dad's gliding stories: the orange haze on the horizon that turned out to be tens of thousands of monarchs, mid-migration; the hawk that landed on the lift strut beside his right elbow, to rest and ride awhile; the student who froze stiff, still gripping the throttle, so my dad had to deck him in the jaw to regain the controls. Once, my father made the mistake of wearing a coat with slash pockets and no zippers. "I was in a steep bank turn at about twenty-five or twenty-eight hundred feet above the earth in the White Bear Lake area. I felt a slight disturbance in my right jacket pocket. And as I looked down I could see my wallet slide out, bounce off the plywood seat that I was sitting on, bounce down on top of the landing gear. I opened the door of the glider—these gliders have doors like old taxi cabs—and I looked down and I could see my blue wallet tumbling, tumbling . . . then I couldn't see it tumbling anymore." FAA regulations demand that the pilot in command have his or her pilot certificate on board. He'd been in compliance on takeoff, but not on touchdown: "My wallet had, essentially, bailed out of my aircraft." Happily, a terrestrian found the wallet in a thicket, like manna, and walked it over to the airfield three days later.

Weather permitting, a glider can travel many hundreds of miles. On cross-country flights, pilots fly circles in thermals to gain altitude, then glide toward their destination awhile, then find another thermal to corkscrew back up. Sometimes, however, there is no next thermal. Sometimes the lift gives out. What happens next is called "landing out."

As my dad explains it, "Landing out means landing in an unimproved area. And 'unimproved area' is a blunt euphemism for 'not an airport.'" In the Midwest, these landings usually happen in a cultivated field, which puts the pilot in a position to introduce himself to a farmer with the news: *Hello, I just fell out of the sky and I owe you some money for the rows of corn I took out on the way down.*

Most of the farmers he encountered were hospitable. "Quite often, before I've been able to get out of the glider, the farmer pulls up on a tractor and says, 'Are you okay?!'

'Yeah, I'm fine.'

'Did you crash?'

'No, actually, I landed here as a deliberate act of will—although I would have preferred to land farther along at an airport—but there was no airport within easy gliding range.'

'Well, how come your plane is tilted?'

'Take a look, it's only got one wheel under its belly, so either one wing tip is gonna have to set on the ground—'"

This is my favorite part of landing out stories, where my dad, a trespasser, has to rebrand himself as traveling circus act.

"'—Hey, would you like to sit in my glider? Do you have any kids or grandkids?'

'Well, yeah—'

'Go get 'em. I got a camera here and we'll take a photo of each one of 'em—you and your wife, all the grandkids, kids.'"

Within twenty minutes, the entire household is swept up in the grand diversion. My dad's ground crew, meanwhile, shows up to begin disassembling the glider and loading it piece by piece into the trailer.

Before leaving, my dad would pull aside the farmer: "If there's damage I've done I'm more than happy to pay for it."

By his report, the farmer's response was usually some variation of, "Damage?! We had a great time! Aah, that'll grow back—come again!"

I've never been one to hang family photographs, but I considered buying a set of paper plans for the Woodstock to put up in my apartment. That set of blueprints would better represent my father than a framed portrait anyway: his face is just an inherited set of features—I don't imagine he feels too attached to it—whereas he *chose* the Woodstock. Plus, I've always liked the look of schematics: the fine lines, the tiny text, the aura of expertise. I imagined my dad visiting sometime, surprised to see his plane beside my books and storyboards. He'd like that, I thought. One night, after some digging online, I found a single set of plans available. Half a bottle of wine later, though, I hadn't gotten around to clicking Purchase. I'd gone down a rabbit hole, reading tips from one builder to another. I found photos of a wide-smiling engineer named Jim Maupin, the principal designer of the Woodstock. *I want to talk to this man*, I thought. I wondered if he'd ever seen my dad's plane—maybe he'd say it was the finest one he'd ever encountered. I poured more wine and started searching for contact information, toggling through several windows at a time. Maybe it could be some sort of gift to my dad, to connect him with Jim directly. On an ancient website, just red text on a black background, I found an email address. But before I could finish composing a letter, I read a post on a message board relaying the fact that Jim "was no longer with us, regrettably." I leaned back in my chair, reading. The post paid tribute to the excellence of the Woodstock's design: "The first time I stalled my n20609, on her maiden flight, I broke out loud laughing. Perfect stall behavior; as mannerly as it is possible to be." *Mannerly*. I scrolled down. The note had been posted nine years ago. By my father.

A few tours ago, worried about the sound exposure onstage, I went to see an audiologist. He outfitted me with a big pair of headphones, ran some tones, and assured me my ears were still pretty good. In fact part of the reason I found the stage so uncomfortably loud was probably *because* my ears were still good. (As musicians lose our hearing, we turn up the volume onstage—a stupid, upward spiral.) European festivals are often carefully monitored for volume, but the kind of concerts Doomtree plays on tour can peak at about 140 decibels. Noise-induced hearing loss starts at about 85. Looking at my scores on the doctor's worksheet, I was enormously relieved.

Not all animals are as vulnerable to noise-induced hearing loss as rappers are. You might think that the birds nesting near an airport, for example, would all be half-deaf. But the little stereocilia in birds' inner ears can grow back if they're damaged. For humans it's all one-way: when it's gone, it's gone.

After the divorce, my dad rented a one-bedroom apartment a few miles from our old house. Maxie and I slept in a bunk bed next to the washing machine in the basement. Flying gliders, my dad earned enough money to help send me to college.

Recently, my father let me read some of his old building notes from the Woodstock days:

Today I will make the aileron spars. I will mill the wood to correct dimension for the left aileron spar and the right aileron spar, and then mill in the correct taper for each spar. Then I will mark the hinge spots and glue on the reinforcing ply doublers and clamp them, then I will make coffee, really strong really black coffee, and then I will drink it.

Cellulose (the strength component of wood) is a sugar, according to my excellent, longtime friend, fellow soaring pilot, and microbiologist Ron McLaughlin. I built an aircraft out of sugar!

He noted that some of the wood he'd used showed 145 growth rings at a depth of 5 inches. That, he wrote, is *Nature's pace of construction.*

Sitting with Leslie at the dining room table, my father and I talked about the arc of his career. His wife, Leslie, is an energetic, successful, semiretired food scientist. They live comfortably in the suburbs—which made my father uneasy for the first few years. He missed the thrill of the hunt at the Goodwill, the dollar-store victories, soldering his own broken things. He'd been proud to make his living the way he did—pulling it almost literally from thin air—and proud to have found a way to live well on modest means. "To be airborne in a motorless aircraft, quite silent, riding air currents that nobody can see; to be able to look up to see sun and moon, to see other birds doing what they're doing . . . to see a storm front coming . . . to see all these things, to me, has been to be able to sort of live like a king."

At the first opening, I interjected, "When you talk about butterflies, you say, 'I see a butterfly.' But when you talk about birds you say, 'I see another bird.' Which, like, implies that *you're* a bird."

His voice caught—he was moved that such a comparison should be considered. "To me they are *the apex* of evolution. It's beyond comprehension that such a finely tuned living creature could have resulted from these conditions that we have on earth."

I'll admit that I don't understand the airborne world the way that my father does, but *apex of evolution*? It seemed like humans might put up a fight for that title. I wondered if his assessment fully considered stuff like satellite communications, strike-anywhere matches, Babylon.

My dad doesn't speak as reverently about anything as he does about birds. But he doesn't go in for a Disneyfied depiction of the natural world either. "I read somewhere, 'Nature is beautiful, but it's under no obligation to be merciful.' When you see a hawk come in and attack the nest of a goldfinch and eat the eggs of the goldfinch and you see the male goldfinch bravely fight the hawk off and then he gets eaten next—I happen to be a goldfinch fan, I love 'em—I *know* the hawk has to eat. I *know* the goldfinch has to eat. It bothers me that the hawk has to eat my favorite bird, the goldfinch. That's nature. Beautiful, yes? Gorgeous creatures? Absolutely. Merciful? No obligation whatsoever."

I wished there were a way to know what these creatures thought of him. I'm not sure if birds can recognize the Woodstock among the other gliders in the sky. And even if they can, it seems unlikely they'd be able to differentiate the wooden kite from the human body inside it.

If my dad spots a hawk while he is driving, he'll lean over the steering wheel, straining to see. He'll mutter some pilot-y observations—*high ceiling, winds from the north-northwest at ten to fifteen knots, alright, alright*—before returning his attention to piloting the sedan.

Driving alone, I've caught myself doing the same: craning to see a bird overhead, squinting into the sunlight. But of course, I have no special meteorological knowledge, so my observations are just vague generalities: *There it is, a brown bird, flying pretty high, but not too high, looks pretty safe.*

Recently, over a round of after-dinner drinks in his living rom, my dad told me, "I made a little compact with myself when I first started to learn to fly in the mid-1970s. I'm going to get a parachute and at the end of my flying career—and the day is now approaching—I'm going to hang that parachute up over the fireplace never having had to use it . . . never having injured anybody, including myself." That sounded like classic Bob Wander to me. The most noteworthy part of the remark was that my dad expected he might one day have a fireplace. But I don't like the idea of my dad staying out of the sky; my whole life he's been part bird.

It occurs to me that when my father stops flying, when he's fully earthbound, the soaring birds will make me sad. But I expect I'll still fold myself in half to watch them circling above me, peering through that little band of blue at the top of the windshield—a little strip of sky held captive in my car. Even if I barely know what I am looking at, let alone what I am looking for, I'll watch them until they're too far away or I've drifted onto the rumble strip.

And even if I'm driving with the windows up, I've got this soft, persistent rush ringing in both ears. Pop, if you gave me that test again, I don't think I'd ever put my hand down now. I always hear you.

The Mirror Test

I recently bought a very fancy tube of lipstick that has to be applied with a small brush and then allowed to set. After that, you can kiss a thousand sailors and drink from all their coffee cups and it will still stay on. It's a matte crimson—pinup stuff that requires a surgeon's hand, no margin of error at all.

I know that one corner of my mouth is a little higher than the other, but I can never remember which side tilts up and which tilts down—I'm too accustomed to my image in the mirror. It takes one of those three-paneled mirrors, the kind you can angle to flip your reflection, for me to perceive the asymmetry. Then it goes off like a car alarm. Looking at the woman, it's impossible to miss the fact that the right side of her mouth slopes downward, making that whole side of her face look like the unhappier half. It's as though she were wearing only one shoe when the feature was installed.

But with my little brush in hand, I can paint us a perfect, level mouth.

The mirror self-recognition test is supposed to determine whether or not an animal is self-aware. The protocol is simple. First, a researcher puts a mirror in the animal's environment and gives him a minute to check himself out. Then the researcher takes away the mirror. Next, the animal is marked with a bit of odorless paint, often bright red. (The animal can't know about the paint, so the researcher has to be real sneaky— or real tranquilizey—about the application.) Finally, the marked animal is set in front of the mirror again. And all the observing scientists lean in, pens hovering over their clipboards. Animals that fixate on the mark and try to remove it are deemed self-aware. Those that aren't interested in it are not. Very few organisms pass this test, and you could probably guess which ones—chimps and dolphins and a few other members of the vertebrate in-crowd.

The mirror test sounds lousy to me. The visual nature of the thing seems to stack the deck in favor of some animals and against others. If bloodhounds had been in charge of the experimental design team, I imagine the test might involve a scented hydrant rather than a daub of paint. And what would it feel like to be fully conscious, but not self-aware? Are we sure that's even possible?

When she first brought me home from the hospital, my mom said she just stared into my face all the time, blissed-out. She couldn't find the line between us—couldn't figure out where her self stopped and my self started.

At two and a half, I understood my mother's given name to be *Mom*. In my first memories of her, she looks a lot like I do now—like I'm a Polaroid that took thirty years of shaking to develop. She typed very fast, did a bedtime hand-puppet routine that enthralled and terrified me, and had a wide smile that reinforced her resemblance to Whitney Houston, who she could match note for note. When I first heard someone at a dinner party call out for a *Sylvia,* I presumed we'd tell this person to keep looking, wish him luck, maybe send him off with a sandwich cut up into little pieces. When my mom responded to that name, natural as could be, I began to suspect the truth—this woman had a secret, double life. *We've known each other for almost three years and you don't even tell me YOUR NAME? You know MY name. How long does it take to get a proper introduction?* She had a whole other self and the nature of the relationship between Mom and Sylvia was unclear. There were, at least, three of us in the room.

Some elephants can't pass the mirror test, which surprised researchers who knew them to be otherwise smart and social. Eventually some scientists asked, *Well, what if they see the red dot, but just don't care about removing it? Or what if they see it, but don't know that it hasn't always been there?* After all, elephant culture doesn't usually involve mirrors; primates are the relentless groomers and self-admirers. There must be more than one way to fail the mirror test: Narcissus didn't fare too well either.

In high school, I read about a tribe of people that slept on the skulls of their ancestors to induce lucid dreams. I was fascinated by this idea; I found a list of techniques that could be practiced during the day to increase the likelihood of lucid experiences at night. I read that hands often look funny in dreams, so I checked my own regularly. I habitually asked myself, *Could I be asleep now?* Eventually the techniques worked— I caught myself in a dream and set about trying to manipulate my environment. I never managed to create a total virtual reality—for me, learning how to drive a dream was like learning how to drive a clutch: the experience sometimes bucked and surged away. But it was a thrill for a teenager who was eager for more control than anyone was willing to cede to her in waking hours.

My most successful dream was set on a sandy island, with dozens of people preparing for a big storm. We were building shelters and gathering food, urgency in the air. Then, as I'd been training to, I realized I was dreaming. And the sight of all those people working together—their fear, their hope and purpose—became very sad. I called for attention. *You're not real,* I said. *This is my dream and you're just figments in it.* One guy asked me to stay asleep as long as I could. I said I'd try. The mood changed from a Habitat for Humanity build to hurricane party; everyone was reckless and sentimental, saying their goodbyes. When my alarm woke me, I felt vacant. Those people, who'd felt like friends, were all gone. And I *missed* them. But those people were just *me,* right?

Years ago, I met a fair-skinned, dark-haired woman who'd recently kicked a meth habit. After she got clean, in the course of a casual conversation someone asked what her favorite color was. She realized she didn't know—the drug had just erased big parts of the person she used to be. So she found some swatches and splayed them out in front of her. And, at twenty-something, she set about choosing her favorite color.

It sounded so strange, like she was a house that had not quite burnt down—whose walls had vaporized, but the paint was left still standing. She was a half self, rebuilding from within: the M. C. Escher hand that draws the other.

The European fire ant can pass the mirror test. Nobody has the slightest idea what to make of that.

In my thirties now, I earn my living as a songwriter and a performer. Usually my job involves singing about intimate, personal feelings—lots of stylized self-expression. However, there are some performance environments in which the objective is to blend voices completely, so that no single singer can be perceived in a unified, choral sound. When I'm working up a vocal treatment with my longtime friend and collaborator Aby Wolf, we synchronize our breathing and worry over every vowel. (*Are you doing that last syllable as* eh? *Or more of an* uh?) Aby is tall and dark-haired like me and when we stand beside each other in rehearsal, our hands lift and dive like sparrows, an improvised notation to express when each note will dip or bend or crescendo. We synchronize our consonants so that the *k*'s all leave the gate at once, like a perfect horse race, and the *p*'s all land together in one little puff, like gymnasts on a mat. I might have spent more time looking into Aby's eyes than anyone else's—while our mouths are busy with lyrics, I watch for a lift of her eyebrows; a friendly blink to reassure me I'm on pitch; or for the hint of strain that means one of us is running out of air. And when we have polished our parts and we are singing them with others in tight harmonies, our voices dissolve into the larger sound. To perceive a single singer—a single self—would only be a distraction, like the black-clad puppeteers just beneath the real show.

After a trip to India in my twenties, I stopped wearing makeup, kept my hair short, and wore plain, shapeless clothes. My mom asked me about it (or maybe I just started sermonizing, unprovoked) during a visit to her mother's house. I explained, "The way I look has nothing to do with my character. I just don't want to get too attached to things that are fleeting. Any beauty I've got is leaving anyway." I went on. She listened. I went on. Finally, she said, "You have a beautiful voice. You didn't earn that. And you don't get to keep it either. So, what? You shouldn't sing?"

You are beautiful for a while. Then you're not. You can sing. Then you can't.

But I didn't want to conceptualize myself as a quicksand pit of changing variables. I wanted something permanent, stolid— a cinder block of a self. Would I be the same me if I couldn't sing? Yes, I think so. But what if I forgot how to read, forgot my name, forgot that I like whiskey, forgot that red is my favorite color? What am I subtracting *from*? Is there some part that can't be ruined by violence, or time, or fatigue? Is there an apple core at the center that stays fixed?

Maybe *self* works like the word *here*—the referent changes as you maneuver through the world. You just drag the word along, like Peter Pan with his shadow sewn to his heel.

The part of the brain that's associated with maintaining a self-concept is at the front of your head (seems right that it should get a prime parking spot). Psychedelics increase communication between this area and a lot of other networks. Scientists think that's why high people talk so much about everything feeling connected. That phenomenon is sometimes called ego death, or ego dissolution, depending on which clique of stoned scientists you're hanging out with.

In relaxing the partition between the self, other people, and the rest of the universe, maybe the chemicals in mushrooms and ayahuasca and other psychedelics daub everything and everyone with red paint, so that we perceive a little bit of self reflected everywhere.

Maybe part of the mirror test is knowing what *isn't* you.

My fancy brush-and-set lipstick cost twenty dollars, which is about fourteen dollars more than I usually pay for lipstick. Totally worth it. The first time I wore it, I shot a little iPhone video to text to my friend Jaclyn. To demonstrate its staying power, I wiped my hand vigorously across my mouth—*Doesn't rub!* But after I watched the video, I didn't want to send it anymore. My mouth looked slanty. My eyes looked old, tired. Irritated at my vanity, I pressed send anyway—that's what I look like, dammit.

During my recuperation from a serious case of laryngitis, my mom came over to my apartment. I pantomimed my half of our conversation or typed out answers on my laptop. While I heated water for tea she sang along to a song on the radio. We often sang together, but it had been a long time since I heard her idly sing a pop song alone.

In its prime, her voice was much stronger than my voice, but the character is similar. I assume that if a doctor threaded a scope down my mom's throat and another down mine, our larynxes would look the same. I've seen footage of vocal cords in action; they look like cartilage orchids. I bet my mom and I would have a matched set. Our spleens probably look the same too. Same with our retinas and the skipping stones of our kneecaps—though maybe hers are lighter because she's older. Maybe I'm not a Polaroid, just my mother's mirror on a thirty-year delay.

Singing with the radio, she did all the little trills I would have, flipped up to a harmony just where I would have. I let the little cart of my voice box move up and down its elevator shaft; I didn't push any air through the reed, but went through all the other motions of singing. Every time I held a note, my mom did too; every time I cascaded down the scale, she cascaded simultaneously. And as the water boiled, I had the surreal sensation that my voice was coming out of my mother's mouth. It was unclear where her self stopped and my self started.

My mother is very religious. I'm not. But I've wondered about how the soul and the self get along.

What if the share of you that went on into eternity—if there were such a share—was not the part that you understood to be fundamental, the part by which you'd recognize yourself as you? After all, it seems unlikely that all of our quirks would make the crossing—am I still lousy with names in heaven? Still easily startled? Will my mother still talk through movies? Will she be seated beside her first husband or the last one? Even if only the good parts are made immortal, who's to say that a trait that served well on earth would be an asset there? Is one benefited by an uncanny sense of direction in heaven? By being able to tie a cherry stem in a neat knot in her mouth? Will everyone have a four-octave voice? Will our avatars be young and symmetrical, or will we simply be relieved of those concerns? If there's a heaven, and it has walls, I doubt they're hung with mirrors. Maybe we wouldn't be able to pick ourselves out of a lineup. Maybe we wouldn't recognize ourselves from any other red-lipped angel passing on the stairs.

Going Empty

I am wearing a floor-length ivory dress with a long, gauzy train. I am also wearing a snorkeling mask and clinging to an orange life ring, floating somewhere off the coast of Mexico. It's day two of a music video shoot. I'm working with a three-man team: the director, DC, is in the motorboat idling nearby; the cameraman, Alex, is swimming somewhere below me with a GoPro in a waterproof housing; and Ricardo, who we call Ricky, is in the water beside me, explaining how this next task must be done. We are constrained by a tight budget, a tight deadline, and the fact that I don't really swim.

Ricky speaks slowly, calmly, and in accented English—English made slightly adenoidal by his own mask. "Right now you are going, like, twenty centimeters below the water, you swim only a little, and then you are on the surface again."

I nod vigorously. I am frustrated and sunburnt and increasingly unable to tell the two apart. In the shots we've done so far, I haven't managed to swim deep enough for Alex the cameraman to swim above me, as planned.

"You must swim *down*," Ricky says. "You must do like

91

this: float on the water with your face down." He holds his tanned hand flat above the water, a little puppet for my body. Then, abruptly, he folds his fingers down ninety degrees. "You bend at the waist. *Then* you start swimming with your arms, and your legs will follow."

I nod. This makes sense.

"Listen. This is not possible to do with air in your lungs." Ricky begins to hyperventilate, to demonstrate the correct technique.

Beneath our lesson, on the sandy ocean floor, there's an underwater sculpture garden. Dozens of human figures, cast in concrete, stand with upturned faces, their blank eyes trained in the general direction of me and Ricky.

An artist named Jason deCaires Taylor has become famous for creating these underwater museums. They serve not only as art installations, but also as conservation projects: deCaires Taylor and his team submerge the sculptures in strategic locations to draw tourist traffic away from threatened reefs. The sculptures themselves are designed to be overcome by aquatic life, eventually seeding an artificial reef as coral grows over the human forms.

I have come here to shoot a music video for a song called "Sound the Bells." In the storyline the director DC and I wrote together, I swim among the statues and eventually become one myself. We've already made arrangements to cast my head in plaster and outfit a mannequin in my dress to shoot her underwater. I've never filmed on location before—the idea would usually be preposterous on an indie budget. But during a recent corporate shoot in Mexico, DC had managed to forge some local contacts willing to take on a passion project. All it took was a few texted images and I was ready to board a plane to meet him there; I'd never seen anything like the underwater exhibition deCaires Taylor had created. I pitched to Lazerbeak with all the persuasive skill I could muster and all parties agreed to a budget of $5,000—more than I've ever spent on a music video, more than I've ever spent on a car. That figure has to cover the airfare for me and the director; the rented boat with the bored captain at its helm; the gasoline for which he will double-bill us; the white dress and the chiffon tacked to it for the train; the aspirin and the sunscreen; the small bribes for the police; the air in scuba tanks; and two days' work from Alex the shooter, who swims below us now, dreadlocks tucked into a neoprene hood, waiting for me to learn to hyperventilate.

What the budget did *not* include was swimming lessons. But back in Minneapolis I have a membership at the YWCA, so for the past couple of weeks I'd been practicing in the pool. At first, I just worked on floating, trying to suppress the trill of anxiety that rang through me every time a wave pawed over my nose and mouth. Then I practiced treading water, panting and swearing at the wall clock. Knowing that I'd have to shoot some scenes submerged, I tried sinking but found myself too buoyant to sit on the bottom of the pool. (At the time, I attributed this failure to the higher fat content in a woman's tissues, even went so far as to blame my breasts for serving as bothersome floats.) Some of my efforts alarmed the Y's teenage lifeguard. While his other wards dutifully swam their laps, the woman in Lane 10 attempted to drown herself in the afternoons—though with mercifully little skill. At the end of my practice sessions, I leaned on the edge of the pool to practice just holding my breath, watching the loveless arc of the red second hand. I held my breath at home too, walking around the apartment, to simulate the oxygen cost of swimming. Even in my one-bedroom, the feel of a spent lungful of air was terrible—without breaking the seal, I'd fill my cheeks with the air from my lungs, then re-inhale it, trying to wring out a few more seconds before panic opened my mouth, a crowbar at my teeth wielded from within.

Ricky takes four fast breaths and forcibly expels all the air from his lungs. He then begins to sink, the waterline rising up the features of his face and then closing over his slick dark hair. That's the trick: I'm supposed to go down empty.

He comes up again, slings his arm over the life ring with me. He says, "Your body, it will do like this"—he simulates a reflex that I know well: the spasm of the diaphragm in an involuntary gulp for fresh air. The sucking reflex tightens the tendons in his neck, deepens the suprasternal notch, the divot where his collarbones meet. But, he says, "This is not because you are out of oxygen. This happens when there is CO_2 built up." Ricky looks hard at me to make sure I understand this distinction. "You will still have more time."

For a recording artist in her midthirties, it's easy to worry about running out of time. Commercial music careers are often very short, singers launch and drop like mayflies. Yet all my life I've been sure—sure that if I sacrificed enough, if I worked through the weekends, through Christmas, through my childbearing years, I'd make it big. I wasn't sure what that meant exactly, but when I committed to becoming an artist, I had an innate belief that if I dedicated myself completely, somehow I'd get the resources I needed to stage ambitious performances; I'd appear on famous stages around the world; I'd make musical contributions of real magnitude; I'd get to talk craft during a heartfelt conversation with Terry Gross while fighting down the thought *I'm having a heartfelt conversation with Terry Gross.*

All that still feels very far away. It's not that my career is in trouble, really: the crowds are steadily growing, the critical reviews are getting better. It's just moving far too slowly. It'd take another sixty years to get where I'm hoping to be, and by then Terry Gross and I will both be dead.

I'm already old for a rapper. Jaclyn told me that a woman's elbows always reveal her age. No matter how fit or trim or smooth the rest of her might look, the elbows don't lie. My eyes, my hands, my tits, they're not lying either—they've all become real conscientious lately. Although I am sleek in this dress, I can really only hold this look for a week at a time. I know how many calories are in a grape, in a stick of gum, in the peanuts they serve on planes. I know that drinking ice-cold water burns calories as your body works to warm it; I know compounds in green tea hold promise as metabolic boosters; I know that grapefruit is sometimes used to suppress appetite. There is an Encyclopedia of Vanities in my head—the only knowledge I'm not proud of having.

I do *not* know, however, how many calories are in the éclairs that they sell at Amoco, because I eat those only after I've given up on counting, alone in my car, sometimes two at a time. When I am home again, after this video is shot, I will put on several pounds before the tan fades.

Santigold had her big break at thirty-seven. I keep that fact in a lockbox for safekeeping but take it out every so often to turn over in my hands. Numbers have no natural predators, they can overrun the mind and choke out other thoughts. If you're not careful, a music career can get reduced to a video game: just a bunch of scores to keep and beat. The headcounts, the downloads, the likes, the streams, the follows, the charts, the stars (is this three and a half out of four? Or five?). Like some sad-case at the casino, you sink your fortune into a blinking machine one coin at a time, and when your hand hits the bottom of the empty paper cup, you are not sure which meal you've most recently missed or if this is how fun is supposed to feel.

Music videos are like little advertisements for songs; they're supposed to be released right before or right after an album drops. "Sound the Bells" has been out for well over a year—it's much too late for any strategic promotion. But I came to Mexico hoping to be defibrillated, to be jolted out of the numeric and back into aesthetic: to let go of all the numbers and be a part of something beautiful. And to let that be an end in itself.

"Here." Ricky hands me a mask. I won't be able to wear it

in the shot, but it will help me review the route I'm meant to swim.

I slip the band around my head and turn my face down into the water, still holding the life ring.

With my feet floating in clear water, many feet above the bottom, I'm struck not by a fear of drowning, but by a fear of heights. Then, off in front of us, I see them, the crowd of people. They are dark figures against the light sand. Coral has already begun to grow on them, softening their silhouettes. Someday they will be the heart of a reef. Tiny particles drift with the current, sparking in the sunlight like fine snow.

Still submerged, I turn to give Ricky a wide-eyed look of awe. He nods and lifts his head out of the water. He's in the awe business.

I hand back the mask and he asks, "Ready?"

He gestures to Alex below; it's time. I take four deep breaths, another for good measure, then press it out, hands on my ribs to squeeze them empty. I close my eyes and float flat, facedown. I bend at the waist. Swim with my arms. My legs go up in the air, like the tail of a whale, then follow me down. And down. Within a few strokes, it's nothing like the fumbling in the pool, trying to stay on the tile. My body descends easily. There are no bubbles because I haven't taken any air with me. My chest begins to burn, but I still have time. My ears suddenly crack, loud and startling. I turn toward the surface and kick. I rise past where the surface should be. My diaphragm spasms. I kick crazily, spending all my oxygen, break the surface, and inhale hard enough to engage my vocal cords with the whoosh of air—making the sound of the animal I'd be if human culture hadn't intervened. My wet hair makes a dark tent around me. I claw it away from my eyes, and spin in place, treading, looking for Ricky. He's close, already bringing the life ring to me. He gives me a smile, the swell of his cheeks dammed by the mask, and a thumbs-up. Once I've gotten hold of the ring, he begins to swim against the current, easy with his flippers, back to where we started. The train in the water billows like a sail beneath me.

"Now we do it again."

Challenging an axiom is like trying to catch a fish by hand—it's tough to get ahold of the thing, let alone lift it out of the water and inspect it properly. Axioms, when they settle into their natural tessellations in our heads, form the paradigm through which we see the world. And looking through your own paradigm is like looking through plate glass: you don't even know it's there until you walk into it, or through it.

In the performing arts, the masterful execution of a familiar idea can be deeply moving—a great performance of a favorite song, for example. But the art that really blows my mind usually violates an assumption I didn't even realize I'd made, eliciting some variation of *Holy shit, I didn't know you could do that*. When David Foster Wallace endnoted the endnotes; when I first heard a backward snare hit; when I first saw a violist play with her bow belly-up, the wooden side tapping on the strings; when Jeff Buckley held that last note of "Hallelujah" for an hour; when I discovered that Sigur Rós wrote lyrics in a language with words but no meaning; when

I first heard an overtone singer throw his voice to the roof of a chapel. Funny thing is, it's possible for a person to learn to do almost all of those things—the hard part is thinking to try them.

All this time at the pool, I'd been practicing exactly the wrong thing. I'd been filling myself with as much air as I could and holding it as long as I could stand to. But really, the trick was to un-hold one's breath.

We take the shot again and Alex the shooter successfully captures footage of me swimming over the statues, my train billowing a few meters over their heads. A passing boat points at me and yells something in Spanish I can't make out. Alex, who's surfaced for a moment, removes his regulator to translate: *Mermaid*. The three of us climb back onto the boat, my sodden train slung over my shoulder like a fourth, drunk companion to head to the last location for the day. In shallow water, less than three meters deep, there's a lone statue of a seated woman. She's been recently submerged, so her features should still be sharp.

The motion of the boat makes me sick. I close my eyes against the rocking horizon. Our captain isn't sure exactly where to find this woman—paper printouts are passed hand to hand, GPS coordinates searched for. I swallow my vomit.

We arrive in the general vicinity of the statue, and both Alex and Ricky swim off to find her. I jump into the water to escape the tossing little boat and the viscous dizziness it induces. Immediately the nausea lifts and I think how strange that the sea would provide a cure for seasickness. A shout turns my head—Alex has found her. The little boat motors over and I grab hold of its small ladder to hitch a ride.

Alex is leaner than anything native to the water—the striated muscles of his forearms more resemble tree roots than the sleekness of a fish. He is from Barcelona but has lived in Mexico for many years with his German girlfriend. In his accent I try to detect this history, like a geologist labeling layers of sediment. "Give her the mask," he tells Ricky.

I dip my face into the water to see the other woman. She is naked, with her legs pulled tight against her chest, arms around her knees. "You know what to do?" I do, we've talked through this shot already.

Alex goes under, camera in hand. Ricky stays above to make sure I don't drift with the current. My right foot catches a bit of coral, a pink puff of blood. I close my eyes. I take several deep breaths, exhale hard. Begin to sink.

When my feet touch the bottom, my knees bend beneath me. I kneel in the sand, facing in what I think is the direction of the statue, hoping I've not turned or drifted away from her. I lean forward and open my eyes to the blur and the burn of salt water. Neither of us can see the other, because one of us is cast in marine-grade cement and the other one doesn't come equipped with the necessary nictitating membrane. But we hold, regarding each other until one of us breaks for air.

At the bar that night, the team drinks mescal, which tastes like tequila that's just finished a cigar. DC, me, Alex and Ricky, and both of their slender women sit at a small bar. Ricky's girlfriend speaks almost no English, but is so beautiful that it's hard not to stare. It takes a compelling man to keep a woman like that.

I let on about some of my recent professional ambivalence. Alex is indignant to hear it—art is a domain for passion, not pragmatism—and in this way he is every bit a Spaniard, with no trace of the mellowing Mexican influence or the reserved Germanic. His long-limbed blonde girlfriend is more sympathetic. She herself chose to dive less, she says, because it took too much out of her. "Like what?" I ask.

"Oh, the wrinkles. The joints start to hurt." Alex leans in to take over the thread of the story as she finishes her third mescal.

"Every diver you see is like this." Alex holds up his pinky.

"Thin," says his girlfriend.

Alex says that the nitrogen a diver breathes underwater stays in his bones at the joints. His girlfriend says it hollows a person, they age early, wrinkle. Since she stopped diving so frequently she has filled out a little. I cannot imagine her having been less substantial than she is now, without pulling teeth.

She says that when Alex stays on land for a couple of weeks, like when they visit her family in Germany, she can see a youthfulness returning to him.

"Ah, but then I miss the water," he says.

Later I'll look up the hazards of deep diving. It's nitrogen that's responsible for the bends, the condition suffered by divers who surface too quickly to properly decompress. The dissolved gases in their blood form bubbles, which can be lethal; the human body is not designed for effervescence. But over the course of a career, even well-controlled dives can lead to osteonecrosis—bone death—and potential damage to the retinas, the ears, brain. I think of ballerinas and their broken toes, pop musicians playing themselves deaf, and the pitchers on the mound who muster enough power to throw their arms apart. There is a price to pay for excellence.

Alex is a good drinker. The rest of us sip and listen. His favorite dive was in the arctic, he says. There, he'd been able to walk upside down in the water, hiking on the frozen ice above him.

Then we drink and listen to Ricky. He was recently hired by a female champion free diver from Chile. He shows us pictures of her in repose in a bikini, lying on the seafloor as if she were a sunbather. He shows us pictures of the human skulls that lie at the bottom of the freshwater caves. He's training to become a better free diver himself, he says, by lowering himself down a guide rope. At sixty feet, it gets easier, he says, because the remaining air in your lungs compresses and "the ocean starts to suck." If you took a breath from another diver's scuba rig while you're down there, you'd die on resurfacing—the air would expand as you ascended, until it burst your lungs.

As the night blurs, DC takes out his cell phone, sets it on the table, and leans back. On it he has queued up a ten-second clip of the shot with me and the statue woman.

We watch around the tiny screen. "Again." Everyone gets to hold the phone and play it once. Ricky is last. He cocks his head to give me a look, holds my eyes to make sure I understand him. The four of us have made a beautiful thing. I do not know if the whole video will be beautiful or if it's only these few frames—and in any case it feels like such a small thing to be so proud of in the presence of ice-walking genuine adventurers—but calculating on six ounces of mescal, five thousand dollars seems like such a small sum to pay for these ten seconds. It is art and it is *good art,* and no, I do not think it will be a sound investment or win an award—though a corner of my heart hopes it might. Living as an artist is fundamentally speculative; there's a permanent uncertainty about where you'll be hired next and how long that work might last. But really that's true of most parts of our lives; the pension, the marriage, the mortgage are all friable, all fallible. We don't own much, and what we do own we certainly can't keep indefinitely. Every breath is borrowed by the lungful; you can't save them for later or hold a single one for long. And even a chestful of air is too much cargo for some trips. Some places you have to go empty.

Life on Land

Before dating my ex-boyfriend, I hadn't considered myself particularly special below the knee. But he liked my feet and that made me like them too. I have unusually long toes, which my *X* called "tingers." (That's not a Pulitzer-worthy portmanteau of toes and fingers, but Pulitzers aren't awarded in the bedroom and at the time it seemed very sweet.)

Our love wasn't good for either of us, but we had a hell of a lot of it. Like a trick candle that couldn't be snuffed out, it kept flaring back to life after the party had dispersed. We caused each other a lot of pain, mostly on accident and sometimes on purpose. The sex, however—probably because of the constant turmoil—was great. Like, outrageously great. If prestigious global prizes *were* awarded in the bedroom, we'd have had a hutch full of statuettes.

Even when he wasn't around, I thought of my toes as tingers. I thought that word when I stepped out of the tub or put on my shoes in the morning. I'm thinking it now, wiggling them in my combat boots.

Loving him made me unhappy, but I couldn't figure out

how to stop doing it. We tried for a long time to make it work, to find some way to keep the affection but ditch the jealousies, the fears, and the resentments. The first time we went to a couples' counselor, she set a throw pillow on the floor and told me to put all of my anger into it (which, of course, put all my anger into *her*). We wrote lists and letters. We phoned late at night to say, "I—I'm sorry. I shouldn't have called." We tried for years to isolate the love alone, but it proved impossible. It was like trying to wring the flight out of a bird.

After many long years of failing with X, I met someone else. He was funny and kind, curious and outlandishly handsome. We dated for several years and together we built something seaworthy, sweet, and affectionate. We began to discover, however, incompatibilities that couldn't be reconciled. He wanted to cook dinners together, make a down payment on a house with a lawn, raise a couple of cool kids. I wanted to tour Asia.

When he and I ended, X's candle flared again, blazed through its box on the closet and threatened to burn down my apartment. I tried one last time to sort it out with X; we went on chaste coffee dates, talked and talked, kissed and watched movies and tried to ease into something adult and viable—and imploded again. I felt mangled and beaten and sorry for myself and stupid to have expected any other outcome. On the advice of friends and books, I made all sorts of rules: Schedule time to cry if you need to, but don't allow yourself to be sad all day. I took his number out of my phone. I resolved to never, ever think about him while masturbating.

But now I find myself in the dumb and embarrassing position in which my own feet make me sad. Even my body reminds me of him. Since our final split, something like a year ago, I've been trying to hide them from myself. I wear socks more often inside, keep my head up in the shower.

In Minneapolis, the city in which we both lived, our lives were threaded together. His friends were my friends. Entering a coffee shop, I'd scan the room to see if he might already be there, small mocha in hand. Idling in traffic, I'd watch for his grey sedan. And then one of his songs would come on the radio and I'd change the station or maybe just let it play and let it hurt. Sometimes one of my own songs would come on: *We've been living too long, too close / and I'm ready to let you go / I'm ready; call off your ghost.* There was no place far enough away from him to properly get over him in Minneapolis. After several months of private deliberation, I decided to rent an apartment in New York. I'd always wanted to live in the city, and if there were any time to go, it was now. I'd figured I'd stay there part-time at first, then decide whether or not to make it permanent.

At a tense Doomtree meeting, I came clean to the whole collective. It was just too hard. I loved them all, but I had to take a break—from everything—or I'd never be able to heal up right. I didn't tell them that I was still struggling to extinguish the hope that X and I might someday reconcile. Hope is incredibly hard to get rid of. And unless you manage to eradicate it completely, it comes right back.

I'd been afraid they'd be angry; I had prepared all sorts of arguments to justify myself. But with patience, grace, and affection, my rap group granted me a sabbatical. The guys told me to take whatever time I needed, to participate how and when I felt comfortable. I told them I couldn't start on any new songs together and didn't want to set off on any big tours, but figured I could manage the occasional one-off.

I flew to New York with an air mattress as my carry-on luggage. I sublet a spot from a drummer slash chef who was a friend of a friend slash stand-up comic. He was going on tour in Australia, so I'd get his Lower East Side apartment to myself. I had just returned from an Australian tour, so I gave him a baggie full of dollar coins on the way out. His apartment had lots of expensive chef stuff and a little Casio keyboard and good water pressure and a few tiny brown roaches that he was in the process of exterminating. I could stay for two weeks, time enough to find my own place.

One-bedroom apartments in New York average something like $2,830 a month. I'd saved up some money, but that figure seemed insane—more than any lovesick musician could reasonably spend on her escape. Every morning I logged on to PadMapper, Zillow, RentHop, and half a dozen other sites. I cycled through the windows all day long, clicking Refresh like one of those research mice who die of thirst because they do nothing but press the lever for cocaine.

Every time a new listing met my parameters, I got an alert on my phone. I'd freeze mid-stride on the sidewalk, a sudden impediment to those behind me, or I'd stop chewing my breakfast sandwich, breathing through my nose while speed-reading the listing, searching for a phone number to set up a viewing. To an onlooker, I might have been a trauma surgeon being paged back to the ER. Every time my phone chimed, I knew a thousand other phones did too. Like a dance troupe whose members would never meet, all the other hopefuls were asphyxiating on their bagels in unison, afraid that if we didn't find something soon, we'd all just have to go back home to Omaha or Tucson or Decatur and submit to the life we'd been hoping to escape.

Racing to one open house, I rushed headlong into traffic, crossing against the light. A car swept past at full speed—the miss was near enough to send a slug of adrenaline through me that left me shaking. *Jesus,* I thought to myself, *pay attention! I don't want to get hit by a car and miss seeing this place.* As if *getting hit by a car* needed a predicate.

A listing for a rent-stabilized unit on the Lower East Side said there would be an open house on Sunday at 2:55 P.M. that would last for five minutes. At the showing, a pale-haired woman corralled in the kitchen yelled to us that *the landlords were LIARS*. Like a diorama at the Natural History Museum, she was the Current Tenant, on display in her natural habitat. The broker told us to ignore her, she was high; she'd been late on rent. The entire scene was unsettling. Within four minutes a fellow renter submitted an application.

In the afternoons, I hit my target neighborhoods on foot, street by street, hoping to find some elderly landlord without a DSL connection who might simply post notice of a vacant room in the window, the way people trapped in burning buildings signal with their bedsheets. On a coffee break, I overheard a handsome black man at a café consider proposing to the cat lady a floor below him because her rent had been frozen at some pre-war rate. I had seven days left to find something.

I caught wind of a fifth-story walk-up sublet for $1,550 a month and arrived twenty minutes early for the showing. A crowd was already milling; people in cars shouted, "What's going on?" A warehouse party? A pop-up restaurant with a Michelin star? Beyoncé? I texted a picture of the scene to my crewmate Lazerbeak back home—he would appreciate the fact that more people had come to see this one-bedroom apartment than had ever come to any concert I'd performed in Florida. On the way up the stairs, I glanced over the railing to see an unbroken line of people, a foot on every stair. It was like the Hajj.

I walked through the unit trying to present as the ideal tenant—someone who listened to music only through headphones, who cooked food with inoffensive smells—a celibate teetotaler with family money and a 9 P.M. bedtime. A few feet away, a deaf couple signed to each other. *Shit, I'm out,* I thought. *They'd be so quiet.* We were asked to a write a short essay about why we deserved the unit. I called twice a day to check on the status of the apartment and eventually learned it went to a gentleman renter. I did not ask if it was his literary style that elevated him among us or if he was deaf.

With only a few days to secure a lease, I abandoned my budget and walked through a spot on the Upper East Side. The floor plan was inexplicable: mostly hallway, like several Tetris pieces melted together, or like maybe the apartment was trying to spell out a secret message. I said I'd take it.

The broker took my application, but said I'd need a guarantor with a yearly income of eighty times the monthly rent. My mom was retired. My dad flew gliders for a living. What if I paid the first few months up front? Nope, they'd want a guarantor. I applied anyway. Then I wrote myself a glowing letter of reference, emailed it to Lazerbeak, and asked him to put it on Doomtree letterhead. The broker wanted bank statements and a tax return. Then a second character reference. I asked my accountant to write a letter suggesting that, even though I was a musician, I was neither drug addled, itinerant, or insolvent.

I ended up sitting in tense silence with the broker and the broker's boss, all of us waiting at a conference table for a final decision to be texted from on high. When the keys dropped into my hand, it felt like I'd been handed a relay baton. It was finally my turn to go—I just wasn't sure who was on my team or which way we were running.

I inflated my air mattress every evening, and every night it deflated gradually beneath me, setting first my hip and then my shoulder on the floor, gently, like a bride. For the first few nights I slept in my clothes, wrapped in a red Delta blanket I'd swiped on the flight over. I was proud of myself and a little scared and perpetually chilled.

Since then I've been gigging hard, earning New York rent. I played a surprise birthday party in Carmel-by-the-Sea—a curtain whooshed open to reveal me and my entire live band, like a car on a game show. I did some voiceover work, recording into my iPhone and hoping the echo of the empty apartment wouldn't muddy the audio. I performed with Doomtree at a handful of one-off festivals. I played a stop on Gloria Steinem's book tour and froze up like a moron when she said I had a pretty voice.

I've been here for five months now. I bought a proper bed, but the Delta blanket's still on it. I do not know how or if I can rejoin Doomtree, but the thought of being a musician without a crew is too frightening to think about too hard for too long, so I try not to.

There's a delivery truck in my new neighborhood that has a huge, realistic painting of a striped bass on the side. Beneath it, there's a phone number for Meat Without Feet. When I first saw it, I thought, *Hey, that's me*. My own feet have been in storage all summer, stowed in black combat boots where they couldn't remind me of X. *I'm just the fish in the second-story walk-up on East Eighty-Second*.

My lease is $1,850 a month. For someone calibrated to the Minneapolis market, that figure is total lunacy. Telling my father I pay that much in rent was like coming out—I stuttered; he tried to hide his confusion and surprise. But he still loves me, even if he doesn't understand my choices.

Not inclusive of the broker's fee, that figure breaks down to $2.57 an hour. That's 4.3 cents a minute, which means I could either lease this apartment or phone Macao on a calling card and leave the handset off the hook for a year.

My first month on the Upper East Side, I mentally converted all of my income and expenses into rental currency. The price of a granola bar at the bodega was the equivalent of twenty-nine minutes in my apartment. Every CD I sold at a show earned enough money to watch a full-length movie on Netflix in my apartment. A plasma donation could earn nearly ten hours in my apartment. By extension, donating *all* of my plasma would net just over four days.

The place seemed way too expensive to leave empty when I was traveling for shows—too valuable to leave empty when I was walking around the block, really. The lease explicitly forbid short-term sublets, but the idea of wasting all that rent was nauseating. I'm the type of person who cuts open empty bottles of lotion. I've brought my own Tupperware to restaurants so as not to waste a box on my leftovers. Everything neurotic and Midwestern about me equates waste with moral failure.

It's that distaste for waste that makes me doubly uncomfortable about the feet thing. I'm fit and young with pretty feet *now*. And I won't always be. Nobody gets to save up their health and beauty for redemption at a more convenient date. Living more or less celibate and alone, I feel like I'm squandering a resource, like part of me is being wasted.

When that thought first walked into my brain, it set off the fire alarm on every floor. *Oh, come the fuck on—you're being wasted? Really? What does that imply you're FOR?* It was antithetical to all of my ideas about independence, feminism, a self-determined life.

But my feet don't know about the male gaze, or joint checking accounts, or conscious uncoupling. My feet haven't read Gloria Steinem.

And to be totally candid, even worse thoughts have darted through. I know that, at least once, I've consoled myself with the idea that when we're both happy with our own lives, X and I might be in a better position to reconcile. As if *being happy with your own life* needed a predicate.

Even on the phone with Jaclyn—my unwaveringly supportive best friend—I tried to limit how much I talked about X. A decade of listening to the same story of reconciliation and devastation would strain anyone's sympathies. And telling it too often was embarrassing anyway. She'd already heard the damn episode. And it sucked.

I talked a lot to myself, though, often out loud in my apartment. Intellectually, I decided that I was completely dedicated to the idea that my youth and my health and my toes ought to be appreciated not by boyfriends, but by *me*. Because I am senselessly lucky to have a body that flexes and functions and moves me through the world. I reminded myself that feet aren't there to be admired. My feet are there to keep my damn body off the ground. And my toes are there to—I realized I wasn't totally sure what toes are for. So I looked it up.

Toes give thrust. And balance. They lengthen our stride, which turns out to be important because humans are actually the best long-distance runners on the planet. I liked that—knowing that we didn't forfeit all of our athleticism when we went bipedal and agrarian. There are still some people around today who hunt by simply running antelope to exhaustion.

So, as it turns out, my toes are there to help me outrun the rest of the animal kingdom. In which case they can certainly outlast the fish in my heart, pining for her bicycle.

The Fool That Bets Against Me

I get a lot of stomachaches. Which means I spend a good deal of time lying on my back on the floor, reading incoming mail. I'm probably one of the few recipients of the Geico quarterly likely to read it cover to cover.

The Geico quarterly is surprisingly well designed. The pages are glossy and the tone is winking—as if the editors are fighting for market share with *Vanity Fair* instead of State Farm.

In a recent article on unusual policies, I learned some multinational companies buy ransom insurance, just in case an executive is kidnapped while working abroad. And that a firm based in London has sold more than thirty thousand policies against alien abduction. Googling, I found two separate companies had taken out a policy on the existence of the Loch Ness Monster, one of them with a payout of over two million dollars.

Springsteen insured his vocal cords, Julia Roberts her smile, Taylor Swift did her legs, Jennifer Lopez covered her ass. In the seventies, Gene Simmons insured his tongue for a million. (I've also heard that he had the connective tissue on its underside snipped, but can't verify it.) David Lee Roth supposedly insured his cock, nicknamed "Little Elvis," before leaving on tour. Bette Davis insured herself against weight gain, with a policy to pay out if she ever found herself unable to lace her corset.

A company sponsoring Fernando Alonso, the Formula One driver, insured his thumbs for nine million British pounds and in doing so spawned a slew of awkward publicity shots in which the handsome face of Alonso is eclipsed by the bulb of his thumb. The digit seems less connected to the rest of his body in every photo—and more like the end of a meaty little baton he's holding in his fist. Non-celebrities got body-part policies too. Some surgeons have done their hands. Chefs and sommeliers and food critics can insure their noses and tongues. A photographer can do one eye.

Years ago somebody at a bar once tried to sell me disability insurance. He was persuasive and I was drinking, but I didn't buy anything. Still, the conversation freaked me out. What *would* I do if I busted my leg or got a vocal node or caught pneumonia and had to cancel a whole tour? Young artists don't think about that sort of thing, he said. And he was right—early in my career it seemed like such a feat to become a working musician that I hadn't spent much time thinking about how I'd fare as a non-working musician. Fear and pain have always been my primary motivators and now, after a decade of different-city-every-night touring, I keep a rainy-day fund just in case a piano falls on me or I fall off a piano. Not enough to go back to school or anything, but enough to float for a while.

If I couldn't sing or rap, I'd always assumed I'd move to

prose, maybe monologue. But the Geico mailer posed a sharp question: On what single asset does my career hinge? That is, what would I insure? All my work depends on a facility with language—but I wouldn't bother taking out a policy on that. Language has always felt so central to who I am; I don't think the rest of me would want to hang around for long if that part of me got torpedoed.

I had a close call with that particular torpedo—aphasia—when I was twenty-three. A tumor necessitated the removal of my right ovary and the subsequent change in biochemistry sent me into a bout of hypomania. I talked too fast, slept too little, crashed a car, and was briefly prescribed lithium. And just like that, the dictionary in my head—usually at the ready—sank to the bottom of a bathtub. I remember riding to an appointment with my mother, slumped against the passenger door with my cheek flattened against the glass, unable to find the word *malaise*. They switched my meds and I got my dictionary back.

But if not language, what? What was singularly indispensable to my career? It seemed like the sort of question a TV life coach would ask her clients—a thought experiment to hone their focus, stoke their drive. Not having a confident answer made me feel uneasy, like I'd be the first one voted off the show.

Then I read about Ben Turpin.

Turpin was a cross-eyed silent film star, a slapstick actor with a signature fall he called the "hundred an' eight." He was phenomenally successful and boasted about it, introducing himself with the phrase, "I'm Ben Turpin; I make three thousand dollars a week." (Even unadjusted for inflation, I can't say the same.)

He starred in movies opposite Chaplin, signed with the leading comedy studio, took the first pie in the face, customized a car with crossed headlights. And whenever Ben Turpin hit his head, onstage or off, he'd rush to a mirror to make sure his eyes hadn't come uncrossed. He insured them with Lloyd's of London: twenty-five grand if they ever went straight. The eyes—they were Turpin's thing.

Bingo. I knew mine.

I write sad songs. Some are funny-sad, some angry-sad, some are dance-even-though(-or-maybe-because)-you're-sad, and some are just sad-sad with all the bells and whistles tuned to D minor. At the beginning of my career, I thought maybe it was something I just had to get out of my system. It turned out to be the only thing in my system. It's what I'm really good at.

I've always run a little blue. I was proud of that as a teenager (I figured it meant I was smart) and ashamed of that as an adult (I figured it meant I was spoiled). Now it's something I expect and accept with less hand-wringing; nobody chooses his or her disposition any more than they chose their eye color. A mild melancholy feels native to me, and although I don't feel it all the time, it's the feeling that makes me want to write. Some people have type A blood; some people have connected ear lobes or can curl their tongues into perfect little cannoli; some people can't remember any of their dreams. We're not uniform by any other measure, so I don't know why we'd expect to arrive on earth with temperaments, all dialed to some universal standard.

My love life adds a circumstantial factor. I've had the good fortune to meet and fall in love with several incredible men. Few of my relationships, however, have lasted long or ended easily. Critical reviews of my records often include descriptors like "wrenching." After I sent my mom the rough mixes of my last album, she said some nice words, then asked, *Why do you always have to make music to bleed out to?* I didn't even know my mom knew that expression.

My relationship with *X* in particular has dogged me—it resurrects and reasserts itself every few years, coming up between the gaps in other romances like a weed I can't spray down. I've tried meditation; I've read *As a Man Thinketh*; I started keeping a journal that I hate writing in; I recorded a bunch of songs about the dude; and I embarked on several money-losing international tours, hoping the hard work and scenic views could clear my head. But the feeling has been tough to shake. For him too.

I think a lot about this relationship (using that term *very* loosely here), much more than I'd like to. Preoccupied by those thoughts, my attempts at happy songs sound forced, like I'm following instructions I found on a cereal box.

The point underscored by Ben Turpin seemed to be that what's good for the organism isn't always good for the artist. The crossed eyes might not be desirable in a man, but they were integral to the comic.

Heartache, that was my thing. Not heart*break*—it's not

sustainably productive. Just a functional, low-grade case of the blues.

I decided to follow through on this idea. Partly to entertain myself, and partly out of curiosity, I wrote Geico directly.

Dear Agent,

My name is Dessa. I'm a Geico auto insurance customer looking to expand my coverage. Your rates are fair, the perforated ID cards easy to tear, and I like the gecko (though I bet I'd hate how much of my premium goes to supporting him).

I read that Ben Turpin insured his crossed eyes because they were crucial to his career. I am a songwriter who makes her living writing torch songs. I'm able to do that well because I'm naturally melancholic and also because of unresolved feelings for a former romantic partner.

If I were to find myself in a state of unchecked, protracted joy, I'd either have to re-career or take a lengthy sabbatical to acquire the skill set necessary for a new mode of self-expression.

Can you please tell me whether or not you'd be able to insure heartache as a professional asset, and if so how much a monthly premium might be?

Thank you,
Dessa.

Geico is a word that starts to look misspelled after the third or fourth time you type it, like maybe the *e* and the *i* might be inverted. But I double-checked: it stands for Government Employees Insurance Company.

After I pressed Submit, I got a message with a confirmation number (2565-CA651JJ9-CA14H) and the note that I could expect a response within twenty-four hours.

If I found a willing insurer, there'd be some important details to hash out. First: How much coverage did I need? Forty thousand dollars felt right. I could live on that for almost a year. Maybe meet some new producers, write some hooks in a major key, get a headset mic—those always seemed like fun.

I'd also have to submit some evidence of the asset. An appraiser couldn't very well be dispatched to my apartment with a stethoscope and a valentine, so we'd need an objective measure of my baseline level of happiness.

I poked around online until I found the name of the thing I was looking for: a psychometric test. I also found a psychiatrist named Matt, who was willing to talk to me the very next morning. I'd only have fifteen minutes on the phone with him, so I kept my list of questions short.

Is there an industry-standard tool for measuring happiness?

Can people game the test—and fake being happy?

What is happiness, really?

Self-satisfied, I packed up my laptop and headed to a neighborhood bar to read an insurance glossary over a glass of chardonnay. The guy on the barstool to my left, many drinks ahead of me, tried making conversation. But he kept getting confused about when it was his turn to talk and when it was his turn to drink.

He brought to mind an important concern, though: the underwriters would want to know about risk factors. What if a stranger charmed me into a fresh romance? Or what if my old flame were to make sweeping lifestyle changes and arrive on my doorstep with a bouquet? In either case, I'd be hard-pressed to turn out a heartbreak song, and therefore in a position to file a claim. But exactly how likely was either scenario? That's the thing with insurance—it's a numbers game, pure and simple. The insurers are just card counters at a casino table, with a poker hand that takes thirty years to play. And the insured, well, we're essentially taking out little bets against ourselves, just in case not everything goes according to plan.

To persuade the guys in underwriting that I presented a manageable risk, I could furnish a record of my romantic history. In fact, my whole family's history could probably help establish my case; there are several divorces between my parents. My dad, who is smart and sensitive, will occasionally announce over cocktails, *Marriage is easy—I do it all the time!* He's a good sport about it now, but I know his romantic relationships have been intensely important to him; I saw him suffer when they ended. After my own breakups, when I'm too full of feels to play it cool at Christmas, he'll say. "Oh, darlink"— he says it like that, like Zsa Zsa Gabor—"I love you. But I don't want to give you advice because, well, I don't have a very good track record on this stuff." Usually he suggests that I talk to the Ingrahams, family friends who *do* seem to have a pretty badass marriage.

Years ago my little brother went through a bad breakup of his own and the three of us sat together, feeling down but tender and grateful for one another. My dad said, "Some families have to be careful about alcohol, or money, or gambling. I think maybe you'll have to be careful about love."

My medical record might further bolster my application for coverage. Technically, after the car crash I'd been diagnosed with cyclothymia: sort of a low-carb version of bipolar disorder, with mood disruptions of a smaller magnitude. I was treated by a man named Dr. Rush, who was perhaps the slowest talker I have ever met. My dad said the doctor himself seemed obviously sedated. Usually slow talkers make me impatient, but Dr. Rush was so kind and insightful that I was glad for the slow drip—his ideas were sufficiently potent that each took a moment to metabolize. I was on a lot of drugs at that point, though, so who knows. In any case, I've got a well-documented history of blue moods.

And even long before having met Dr. Rush, when I was still a flat-chested fourteen-year-old, I remember deciding that I wasn't overly concerned with happiness. I didn't want to be *un*happy, I just wanted other things more. Mostly to get really good at making art. And if I had to trade in some happiness poker chips for art poker chips, I was glad to make the exchange.

Within twenty-four hours I got a rejection call from Geico. On the phone an operator said they only did general liability insurance for commercial clients. But that I could try again at a later time because they're still growing.

I'd expected as much; Geico's policies stay on the straight

and narrow. I figured I'd try Lloyd's of London next—those are the guys into weird stuff. They've insured beards against fire and theft.

As scheduled, Dr. Matt the psychiatrist called. He sounded young.

We dove into my questions and Matt proved to be a trove of information. There are a lot of tests for happiness, it turns out. Most of them have names like Bandcamp download codes: PHQ9 and the like. There was also one called PROMIS (which irritated me more the longer I looked at it—Patient-Reported Outcomes Measurement Information System—couldn't they add *Evaluation* or something to finish the damn thing?). Matt said he'd email me one. But, he said, he was actually way more interested in quality-of-life measures than a happiness score or even in specific symptoms.

Matt treated mostly schizophrenics who'd just had their first psychotic episode—which he described as a very treatable group. But where the standard questionnaires asked questions like, *How often are you hearing voices?* and *How loud are they?*, he emphasized the question *Are you living how you want to live? Going to work or school, having good relationships?*

"When I'm dosing medication, I don't go up until the voices have gone away," he said. "I go up until my patients can live the way they want to." I decided I liked Matt. I was also fascinated by the idea that auditory hallucinations came with volume knobs.

I asked, "Do you think of happiness and sadness like light and dark—sadness is where happiness isn't? Or is it like red and blue—where they're both distinct entities?"

"If I could answer that eloquently, I'd probably be in another line of work."

Fair enough. More my job, I guess.

But, he explained, "I don't *treat* sadness—sadness is something we all feel, we have a right to feel, and we are obligated to feel. Depression," on the other hand, "is a pathological state."

Unprompted by me, he brought up the human appetite for sadness in art: "How many people have rented *Steel Magnolias*? And they somehow enjoy it."

"I *know*! Most of my songs are really sad—"

"Yeah," he said loudly. "They are."

I was flattered he'd listened.

When I asked if it was possible to game the test and to fake being happy, Matt said he wasn't sure why anyone would do that. I did not tell him about Geico.

Before we got off the phone, Matt had something he wanted to add, to contextualize our whole conversation. "We're all trying to pick up the pieces from Descartes," he said. "The whole mind-body dichotomy is false. We're a big meat bag powered by a meat computer. If anybody tells you it's all in your head— well, yeah, where else would it be?"

Matt for President, as far as I was concerned. We hung up and he emailed me a PROMIS.

Descartes was a douchebag in a lot of ways, but I admit I'd always kind of liked his mind-body stuff. I studied philosophy in college, and reading Descartes made it sound like you got to keep your mind clean, in a ziplock baggie, out of the muck the body had to wade through.

Earning a philosophy degree involved a lot of thought experiments. We were always pulling ethical levers on train tracks or harvesting one healthy patient's organs to distribute to a dozen other sick people, that sort of thing. One hypothetical in particular stuck with me:

Imagine you're in a loving, monogamous marriage. You've got a good job. You're happy. Then one day a stranger tells you that your life is not what it has seemed: your spouse is cheating on you, doesn't love you at all. You can learn your true circumstances or the stranger can erase the conversation from your memory, *Men-in-Black*-style, and you can continue as you were, happily.

It's essentially a romantic version of the red-pill/blue-pill thing: *The Matrix* meets *The Notebook*. And despite how much everyone talks about happiness, I think the majority of us sides with Keanu: we want something even more than we want to be happy. We want to have an authentic experience— to understand our lives, even the sad, lonely, and unsolvable parts.

For most of my life I'd presumed, without much consideration, that being sad meant I was doing something wrong. My brain was making chemicals in the wrong ratios and I was doing a bad job at falling in love and then when it was time to fall out of love, I couldn't jump out of the damn plane when everyone else did. But maybe my sadness wasn't just a failure to be happy. Maybe it was a feeling I should try leaning into for a while.

Fortified by my conversation with Matt, I wrote my letter to Lloyd's of London.

Dear Lloyd's of London Representative,

I am a songwriter looking for a line of commercial insurance. I make my money writing torch songs and I'd like to buy insurance against a makeup with an ex. (I believe the policy would fall under the Disability category, but I think it's best conceptualized as the opposite of Divorce Insurance.)

Most of my writing runs on heartache—an asset that I believe can be fairly appraised. I've attached a psychometric tool called a PROMIS here.

I'm looking for $40,000 in coverage, to be paid out in the event of a romantic reconciliation that renders me unable to perform professionally in my current line of work.

The likelihood of a settlement, however, is very low. He and I have had many years to sort ourselves out and we haven't managed it. I've recently moved across the country, in fact, to prevent any chance encounters. I live in a stamp-sized apartment now on the Upper East Side and everything in this place I carried up the stairs myself—I'm just stacking up nightstands to make a chest of drawers.

The guys at the thrift store greet me by name; I found a Latin bar that I like; and I spent forty dollars at Staples on a huge pad of Post-it notes—I papered the whole kitchen with them, so every time I have an idea I can just pick up a Sharpie and write it on the wall. I'm just a little bit blue, which some people think makes a person self-absorbed, but I don't find that to be true; I feel sensitized to other people's sorrow, like I've got night vision. I still think of him every day, but the crying jags are over and the dreams about him have stopped or I have stopped remembering them. I bought a keyboard on Craigslist and I'm working long hours, trying to make some music out of this feeling again. It's a delicate process that's easy to screw up, like a soufflé or a house of cards, but I know the steps to this particular kind of alchemy very well. It's as though I'm sitting at a spinning wheel in a room full of hay. And I am the maiden, with her work laid out before her, and I am Rumpelstiltskin who comes to her aid, and I am the heartless king who put her there in the first place, and I am also the hay.

Thanks for your time and consideration. If the premium is affordable, I'll look forward to working with you.

Sincerely,
Dessa.

After a few days without a response to my letter, I decided not to send a third. It's monastic and it can be a little lonely, but I'm living how I want to live. And if I find myself beset by an unexpected bout of happiness, well, that's a risk I'm willing to take.

Slaughter #1

The morning of my mom's first slaughter, I was twenty-nine, a pescatarian, and living on a rapper's schedule—I wasn't usually out of bed at 9 A.M., let alone outdoors, communing with the allergens. But I stood beside her, squinting in the sunlight, waiting for the slaughter guy to arrive. On the other side of an electrified fence, her small herd shaded beneath a stand of trees in the distance. She'd been raising cattle for less than a year and I got the sense she was anxious about the big day. I'd made the ninety-minute drive from Minneapolis to offer a little moral support. I was also morbidly curious; I'd never seen a complex organism die, let alone be killed. Death isn't usually an event you can pencil into your day planner. Over the phone, Mom had explained that the slaughter guy would come to the farm and do it right there in the pasture. In a matter of minutes, he'd kill the steer, skin it, and butcher it in the open air. Most of my male friends thought he'd be using some sort of superpowered air gun, like the kind in *No Country for Old Men*. My female friends all supposed he'd just slit the steer's throat.

My mom has since become an accomplished cattlewoman, but the learning curve that first year was steep. In the spring, she'd tried to castrate a female calf. She and her husband, David, had barely managed to confine their little bulls—and one misidentified heifer—in the handling area when the hired man pulled up to perform the castrations. He made quick work of the first bull and the second, but then reaching in to do the third, he announced, "Wait a minute, this a two-holer."

My mom decided to become a cowgirl in her sixties. I didn't love the idea. She'd grown up in tenements in the Bronx, a New York Puerto Rican, and had worked in offices her whole life. During my childhood, we'd raised only gerbils and did even that badly. I'd dropped one when it was still a newborn and ruined it so that its neck bobbed in circles whenever it walked. My mom knew it had to be put out of its misery, but couldn't bear for either of them to face the job sober. She drugged the broken thing with red wine before taking it outside with a cleaver. To my knowledge, that was her only slaughter to date.

But growing up in New York, she'd always dreamt of living on the prairie. She read the book *Silent Spring* and became an environmentalist before there was much of a movement to join. She'd left the city as soon as she had the chance, locked it down with my dad, and bought a house in Minneapolis to do the middle-class family thing. She tilled our backyard until it was nearer a field crop than a garden. She dehydrated everything that wasn't bolted to the floor.

By ten, I'd learned to dye my own muslin in beet juice in

the backyard. I planted sweet corn (because it was the closest thing to candy that grew out of dirt) and morning glories (because a flower that could open and close and climb fences seemed at least partially self-aware). I quilted at the Minnesota State Fair and knew most Amish designs by name. There is more than one picture of me in a bonnet. I was sometimes a reluctant participant, but was also an arrogant quilter—my piecework was on point and I knew it.

Sitting in the kitchen with me and my brother, my mom loved to imagine what it would have been like to live in Laura Ingalls Wilder's era: the heated stones we'd use to warm our frozen bedsheets, the preserves we'd eat during winter months. Her face would brighten as she listed all the things we wouldn't have. Survival was her favorite game; her dream house would have been made of sod.

She was only a naturalist on nights and weekends, though. Working in communications, she was all executive polish. She wore a dot of Chanel No. 5, black-and-white fitted suits, and small pearl earrings. With long limbs, a narrow waist, and wide-set eyes, she was more beautiful than I would become. Like most people, I just liked looking at her: a Puerto Rican gazelle right there in the kitchen and in a darted blazer.

Mom had been canning and quilting and catching wild yeast for sourdough starters since before I was born—when those were still things poor people did, before the Great Pinterest Revival. As I became an adult myself, the amplitude of my mother's enthusiasm for grassland was mysterious to me; prairie is just what happens when you miss your exit. The rap career I was building was not culturally compatible with homebrewed mead or stiff-brimmed bonnets. I toured too much even to keep a houseplant. (Though I tried once to take a basil plant with me on the road. I named him Milagro, *miracle* in Spanish, and he died in my cup holder.)

My mom was already divorced, remarried, and nearing retirement when she started talking about grass-fed beef. She was such a slight, elegant thing—so easy to imagine crunched, that the idea worried me. I was afraid she'd get kicked or trampled (which is really just kicking without malicious intent) or that she'd just burn through her retirement money and go broke trying to be a cowgirl.

My opinion, however, was not solicited. One December evening, on her commute to her country home, my mom saw a herd grazing on the side of the road. She thought, *Those are the kinds of cows I want for my farm.* She'd lived modestly for most of her life and had some money saved up for exactly this bovine ambition. She pulled over, knocked on the door of the nearby farmhouse, and asked the eighty-year-old woman who answered if she'd be interested in selling. The elderly woman, who declined to open the screen door, said her husband would have to answer that question—and he was out in the field. My mom, still in her corporate attire, slid a business card in along the doorjamb. On her way back to the main road, she saw the lanky farmer coming in. She headed him off and made an offer right there in the snow. He agreed to sell her five bred cows and one steer. She wrote down the price in a tiny mileage notebook, and asked him to sign the page.

To me, this whole story was like one step above magic beans.

A week later, the cattle were delivered. My mom wrote press releases by day, then changed into work boots at night to mend fences, dig holes, bale hay. She got a big belt buckle. A John Deere hat. And I remembered what it was like to start rapping, when every trapping of the culture was a fresh thrill—*Here I am checking a microphone! Here I am in the middle seat of a tour van on the way to OMAHA! Here I am making a thoughtful face in a real mixing studio, pretending to hear a difference when that guy turns the black dial!* Even the problems were exciting at the beginning: the cost of hay for her, the delays at the vinyl manufacturer for me; the ill-tempered cows, the sleazy promoters. Complaining is a special pleasure for initiates: it's proof you're too familiar to be awestruck anymore; it divides the hobbyist from the glory-worn professional. And it's intoxicating to hear yourself begin to sound like the thing you'd hoped to be.

On the morning of that first slaughter, the lone steer was slated for harvest. She'd named him Burger. He was now twelve hundred pounds and dark brown with a white stripe around the middle, where a cow would wear a corset. Her breed is called BueLingo and they all have that middle stripe; her neighbors called them Oreo cows. Meat from this first harvest wouldn't go up for sale; she and David would cook it at home and share some with the neighbors. The slaughter guy, when he arrived, would get to keep the hide.

"Should I call them now?" my mom asked. "They could walk off before he gets here."

"Then don't call them now."

She handed me two cameras, one for stills and one for video. I was supposed to document the occasion for her blog. To promote the farm, she had started a website, a Twitter feed, a radio show, and would eventually print up business cards with a QR code and the tagline *Farming with a tiny carbon hoof-print*™. I was both impressed and distressed that my mother seemed to know more about podcast distribution networks than I did.

"Boy, I wonder if I should start calling them."

"Mom, do not call the cows yet."

My mom spun her wedding ring with her thumb and squinted at the cattle. "Okay."

I wanted to do something nice for her, but my allergies were starting to kick in, and allergies make it hard for me to be nice to anyone.

My mom surveyed the field, presumably seeing a world of small chores that were invisible to me. I knew she had to roll the hay into bales, but I didn't know when in the season that was supposed to happen. I knew some of the fence posts needed replacing, but couldn't tell which ones. And I knew that she and her husband were forever at war with the stones. Their land was very rocky, a problem for bladed equipment. So with bowed heads they walked every acre to find, heft, and set aside the large ones. When they were done, they'd start again; the heavy grey rocks pushed up through the topsoil continuously, unstoppable. Although my mom had described it with only mild irritation, the prospect of this particular duty horrified me—endless, eternally unwinnable. I wanted to say, *You know there's a famous story about that, right? About a guy who has to push a rock forever?*

When the slaughter truck arrived, we discovered it was actually a two-man team: Slaughter Guy and Helper Guy. They pulled up in a flatbed pickup, rigged with a little crane in the back. Slaughter Guy wore a grey T-shirt, pulled taut around his belly, thin from wear and washing. He carried a .22 rifle and a thin, curving blade. Helper Guy was smaller and moved laboriously. He spoke only to his employer and did not make eye contact with women.

Slaughter Guy asked earnestly if my mom and I were sisters, to our respective delight and bitter sadness.

After introductions, Mom set out into the field at a fast march, carrying a bucket of corn and a bell. I fumbled with the video camera, afraid to miss the magic moment when the cows were enchanted by her bell and feed. Slaughter Guy said, "Ha. A *camera.*"

It's a petty hang-up, but I *really* don't like being dismissed. By anyone at all. Doesn't matter my opinion of them.

"She's got a website about the farm," I said. I hooked my fingers through imaginary belt loops and announced in a pretend homesteader's voice, "I'm just the lowly city kid come home to point the camera." He laughed—score. I was back in Slaughter Guy's good graces. I knew my role in this scene: I was a woman in Converse High Tops, obviously in the throes of a serious hay fever, who had tucked her yoga pants into her socks in a last-minute panic about ticks. I was not the boss here, was not a member of the in-crowd. But, having shown Slaughter Guy my underbelly to acknowledge our respective hierarchical positions, we could now resume amicable relations appropriate to our relative status. I confided in neither Slaughter Guy nor Helper Guy that I did not eat red meat.

My mom began to sing a little cow song, which sounded like it had been transposed from a baritone register. She spilled some feed, rang her bell. The cows kept their distance, snubbing my mother's offered charms. The low-battery signal flashed on my camera. I suspected my mom might be feeling embarrassed in front of me and the guys, didn't want to look like a rookie. Slaughter Guy interjected with an explanation to save her farmer's honor: "Well, I don't think they're coming; they knew it's us." I didn't hide my wonder in asking him, "Can they really tell it's you? Is it the smell of the truck?" He wasn't sure exactly how, but he seemed to think that on some farms, particularly those he's visited before, the condemned were wise to his purpose.

He reassured my mother, "If they don't want to come close, I just get the big gun and shoot the son of a bitch." He pulled the rifle out of the truck. This was not the type of language likely to endear Slaughter Guy to my mom, but I was warming up to him.

"Which one is it?" Slaughter Guy asked. My mom pointed to Burger, his large head down and grazing, his herd tight around him. Slaughter Guy loaded his gun, then hoisted himself into the flatbed to take aim. He would have to shoot through the cows to hit his target, like a sniper aiming at the bank robber with a hostage in his arms. I wanted to stay close to the action; my mother kept urging me back. I watched Slaughter Guy aim for what seemed like a long time, then the gun bucked against his shoulder and issued an echoing crack. My eyes raced to the herd—they were running again. *Did he hit Burger? Where the hell was Burger?* I berated myself for watching the gun; I should have been watching the steer. But yes, Mom confirmed that Burger was in the grass. It struck me as strange that we didn't hear him fall, that such a heavy thing could go down without a thud. We started toward the carcass.

The steer was well shot, right through his big, dark head. Slaughter Guy's previously cavalier demeanor was replaced by a shrewd taskmaster's as he issued crisp directions to Helper Guy. At this point in the process, speed became important. The faster the carcass was quartered and hauled off, the less meat would have to be cut away from the surface to prevent flies and other nasties from contaminating the meat.

The two men ran hooks through the steer's rear ankles. Using the crane mounted on the truck, they hoisted the carcass into the air so it hung upside down, tongue lolling, blood draining into the grass. Hung that way, the steer made a rough crucifix against the sky. It looked like he had somehow flipped into the air with uncowlike agility—frozen in one last leap. The steer's belly was slit, his corset opened, so that Helper Guy could pull his guts onto the ground. They came out in one neat package; there was some sort of membrane holding them all together, as if he has been pre-bagged, conveniently designed to come apart. Burger was decapitated and skinned.

Eventually he was chainsawed down the center, so that his two halves swung freely, difficult to reimagine whole.

I'd been bracing for the nausea to roll in, but stayed steady in my Chuck Taylors. When I'd given up meat years before, I'd done so for moral reasons, after watching a college professor present a logical proof for vegetarianism on the chalkboard. The thrust of the argument was: it's wrong to cause needless pain. Animals raised for harvest live in uncomfortable, painful conditions. And we could totally subsist on pasta and salad. But this animal had it pretty good, I thought. He never saw it coming. The pain argument didn't really hold here. I decided it'd be alright to eat the meat my mother raised; I would eat Burger.

I didn't know it then, but pain can be difficult to detect in cattle. My mom, now with years of experience, has explained to me that, "Prey animals tend not to show pain—that would make them an easy mark for a predator." To discern which animals might be suffering from injury or illness, she has to be the steward capable enough to see through their stoicism. And she can do that now—she can do all sorts of cool farmer stuff like gauging a bull's fertility by assessing the "testosterone hump" on his back or calculating how much feed hay she'll need based on the ambient air temperature. She's president of the board, in fact, of the country's largest organic farming conference. But in the moments after that first slaughter, I was just worried maybe she'd feel like she'd hired a hitman in a threadbare T-shirt to assassinate her guy Burger.

I stole a quick glance, looking for some small clue as to how she might be holding up. She was a tough read, standing in her work boots, mouth set. Her crow's feet were evident in her sternness; she's lucky to have the good kind that sweep gracefully, like they were done by a calligrapher.

Most of us, I think, suspect we know our loved ones better than they know us. Maybe that's borne of collective conceit, a compliment to our own powers of perception. But I think there are acres of my mother that I don't have access to. She's always been affectionate with me and Maxie, but also private. And proud. In her corporate life, she maintained an impenetrable firewall of professionalism. Big displays of emotion could make you ineffectual, she said. Even at home, she was sensitive to roles: she'd often put down my whining with "I'm not your friend, I'm your mother." I've inherited some of that thinking from her: I don't like to talk in public about my problems until I've solved them, don't like to share rough demos. I go to great lengths not to appear vulnerable or overtly emotional in my professional transactions. Even with my mom, I minimize my vulnerability when I can: I remember sitting in her sewing room as a girl, making my first bra out of black Lycra and elastic to spare myself the embarrassment of having to ask for one. But in the lyrics and the essays I write, I blow most of the doors open. It's not that I have a particular interest in confessional art—it's just that true stories are boring if you skip all the embarrassing bits. My mom posts my new music on her Facebook page, and every once in a while she includes a caption, something like, *Oh you got me with this one my girl*, so I know that something in the lyric resonated with her. But of course she's not writing emotional rap music about her own life that would allow me to peek over the fence of our relationship and into the parts of her that are not involved in mothering me. If she ever talks out loud and at length about her biggest hurts and fears, I think it's probably while saying her prayers.

When a friend in Minneapolis found out about my mother's farm, she'd rushed to tell me about her own farming childhood; her parents' barn was charged with emotion—lambing season was full of cooing, the slaughter full of tears. That surprised me a little. I'd expected most farmers would be calloused to their work. But love and loss are always natural partners. On a farm, you can start loving whenever you like, but you will be losing at 9 A.M. on the first weekday in September. There are two schools of response to that prospect: to delay the loving as long as possible, to lessen the pain of the losing, or to start loving immediately to get as much of it in as you can before the losing starts. I was pretty sure, though, that my mom's perspective wouldn't be so sentimental—more informed by the *Farmers' Almanac* than *Charlotte's Web*.

My mother says she doesn't love the cows. And I believe her. But I know there is *something* that she feels, some connection. If seeing Burger butchered caused her pain, she didn't show it. She was watching, learning, set to excel in her new role.

"That'll be sixty-five dollars," Slaughter Guy announced. I tried to keep my face expressionless on hearing this alarmingly low number. How on earth did they make a living killing for that?

My mom reached for her checkbook. A hybrid feeling hit

me, both tender and proud. Everyone, including me, had tried to dissuade her from this ambition. And she'd persisted. My mom was badass. Also, there was a satisfying symmetry to it: Mom was born in the Bronx to become a rancher and I was born on the plains to become a rapper.

My mom cut the check, free now to tend to the remaining herd. I was free to return to the city and re-up on Claritin. Burger would spend the next weeks in a meat locker, waiting for an appointment with the butcher.

Slaughter Guy, presumably, would head to another farm to earn the next sixty-five. I wondered what he was like in his personal life—if all these years of slaughter had crystallized some understanding of death and loss unclouded by a civilian's sympathies. What had he said to his son when the family dog died? If his wife left him, would he announce, "No use crying on it" and then go slaughter something with his usual blasé? And after all his years in the trade, would he anticipate his own dispatcher, cued by some familiar scent? I would bet good money that Slaughter Guy did not like doctors, sanctimonious with their scythes small enough to fit in the breast pocket of a crisp, white coat. Maybe he'd submit with less resistance than the rest of us to the summoning bell.

Daylight in New Orleans

This is a classic work-hard, play-hard hand." Miss Kristen read my palm by the light of her iPhone 6s. We sat tucked together into a corner of Hex: Old World Witchery in New Orleans. She'd pulled a curtain around us for privacy, creating a dim office roughly the size of an airplane bathroom. My palm, illuminated by her screen, was like a tiny, spotlit stage. Miss Kristen had blunt-cut bangs, like mine. She wore a black top with a low, scoop-neck collar and billowy sleeves. Her purple glitter nail polish was chipless, but based on the crescent of bare nail between cuticle and paint line, I'd guess it'd been six days since the last coat.

I do, in fact, consider myself a work-hard, play-hard sort of girl. But I'm pretty sure that's as easily divined from the lines around my eyes as it is from the lines on my palm.

I am a woman in her midthirties with dark hair, olive skin, and a gap in my teeth wide enough to swipe a credit card. I've spent many years now as a touring performer, rapping and singing on the road. The benefits of the job are easy to guess: you get to travel the world with your friends, make music you believe in, dress anyway you like. Sometimes you get fan mail or free drinks or a standing ovation. There is, however, an adventure tax. Unless you live with other, non-touring people, you may not be able to keep pets, houseplants, or perishable food items. You will probably miss birthdays, weddings, and possibly the funerals of people you love. While a national tour can hit forty cities, you might not actually see much of them. The indie musicians I know spend most of their daylight hours in transit when they're touring. We lunch at roadside fast-food joints, stand in line behind one another at gas station bathrooms, then roll into town just in time for load-in. By the time the stage is set, the museums are long closed; the bookstores and thrift shops are settling up for the night too. It's easier to crowd surf than to get a walk-in haircut on tour. Work and play are both hard, and sometimes hard to tell apart.

Miss Kristen tucked a Tarot card into the crease where my fingers met my palm. All my fingers joined my hand in a neat line, except the pinky, whose seam sloped toward my wrist. "That's called a dropped Mercury." It indicated a propensity to tamp down my own desires, give too much to others.

Well, who doesn't want to hear that her biggest flaw is generosity? And the implicit prescription for self-indulgence—that's gotta play well with anyone visiting the French Quarter. People come for the party: cocktails in to-go cups, late music, rich food, boys, girls.

Travel was important to me; she could tell as much from the striping on the side of my hand. "There's a lot of chaining on your heart line." Miss Kristen's nail traced the arc of hatch marks that meant I didn't have a clean romantic trajectory.

Well, that was uncontestable. I thanked Miss Kristen and took her card. She asked for a positive review on TripAdvisor.

I started touring through New Orleans almost ten years ago, playing venues like One Eyed Jacks, House of Blues, and Tipitina's. Most of my experience of the city has been nocturnal. If I spliced all of my waking hours in New Orleans into a continuous reel, it would play like footage from an arctic observatory in the dead of winter—many hours of darkness, then a flash of sunlight before the next twenty-hour night began.

After years of frequent but brief visits, I know most major American cities the way that I know my postman. I know that in Pittsburgh they say *yinz* instead of *y'all*. I know that the thrift stores in DC are full of diplomats' dresses, barely worn. In Atlanta, there's a speakeasy that charges one hundred dollars for a martini—because it's rimmed in cocaine. New Orleans, to my knowledge, is the only city in which I might have performed on a stage below sea level. That's a metabolic boon for a vocalist. In Colorado, by contrast, the altitude can wreak havoc on a rap show. If you don't pace yourself, it's easy to end up gasping and exhausted halfway through the set, with a five-drink slur from three light beers. On Doomtree's last pass through Aspen, the club kept an oxygen tank side-stage so we could get a decent lungful between verses.

This time I wasn't in New Orleans for a gig. I'd arrived

alone to write an article for the *New York Times Magazine*—
my first big-league writing assignment. I'd get to see what the
city looked like open, with kids and commuters, sun and sober
pedestrians. I'd get to select my own meals and eat them sitting down, in a chair I wasn't belted into.

My flight landed midday and a split screen opened in my
head, with the routine I'd be running if I were on tour. I ate
lunch on Frenchmen Street at the time of day I'd usually still
be on the road with the rest of the crew, waiting my turn to
plug my phone into the cigarette lighter adapter. At dusk, I
stood on the wooden footbridge in Louis Armstrong Park—
an hour when I'd normally be unloading bins of merch from
the van. At eight I'd usually be standing on the tops of my
own boots, changing into show clothes in the bathroom, but
instead I was on the St. Charles streetcar, headed uptown to
attend a concert myself.

I arrived at the Maple Leaf Bar too early; techs were still
wiring the stage. I'd never performed there, only read about the
venue as a reliable spot to catch solid local players. The bar was
simple—dim and well-worn—while the rest of the street looked
comfortable: an upscale grocer, a well-lit head shop, a gym of-
fering aerial yoga. I ducked into the sushi spot next door, feeling
a little lame about eating Japanese in New Orleans.

The man who sat beside me at the bar had curly hair and a
ruddy complexion. He had a cleft chin when he was straight-
faced. Smiling, it ironed itself out. He was Cajun, I'd learn,
and looked to be in his forties. His name was Doug and he was
a drummer.

We did what musicians do when they meet each other—we

recited our respective tour routings and discographies until we found a point of intersection. We landed on Dave Pirner of Soul Asylum. Doug had rehearsed with him; I'd been considered for an opening slot on a tour that didn't quite pan out. We traded notes on clubs (Doug liked the Dakota in Minneapolis) and favorite cities (we'd both been blown away by Istanbul). Later I'd try to remember what his hands looked like, if he had travel lines like me.

By his tally, Doug had played 110 tours through Europe. On his first trip, "All I knew was the term *Europe*"—he gestured at an imaginary map—"I didn't even know what was in there." A couple of hours into the flight he'd flagged down an attendant to ask, *Excuse me, are we almost there?* I laughed.

For Doug, the musical capital was clearly New Orleans. It was here, he explained, where all pop music really started. "The Nola groove is based on that clave," the Afro-Cuban beat. This was *the home,* he said, of "skeleton rhythms." I told Doug I'd never heard that term. He was graceful, but I think for him my ignorance of the phrase was akin to a purportedly professional musician who'd never seen a piano. *Aah, I see—it's like a harp, laid flat to be played by typewriter?*

As he described the roots of New Orleans music—the Creole influence, the Sunday songs in Congo Square during the slave era—Doug leaned forward on the bar, like a bad card player with a good hand. Almost every New Orleans musician I met was like that: reverent, eager to recount the lineage of the sound. Musicians are usually self-promoters, more likely to give you a download card than a cultural history lesson.

In my own career, race and music have always been linked,

and often uncomfortably. My mother is Puerto Rican, but I'm light enough to be ambiguous, or to be mistaken for completely Caucasian. When someone asks what I do for a living at a dinner party, and I answer, a corporate type will usually cross his arms in a half-assed B-boy pose and ask, *Like, rapper-rapper?* If he happens to be wearing a cap, he will turn it backward at this point. When I confirm—*yes, a rapper-rapper*—the guy will often recruit a friend to the conversation to share in his astonishment. I will readily concede that I don't look the part (particularly if I'm wearing either bangs or glasses) and, yes, incongruences are interesting. But I often get the very strong sense that part of this guy's flabbergastedness is due to the fact that I'm socially polished and well educated—traits he doesn't expect from rappers. And maybe, by extension, traits he wouldn't expect from young black men in street wear. On the other hand, I don't have license for much righteous indignation. I didn't grow up immersed in rap culture, wearing out N.W.A cassettes and tagging my notebooks. I grew up dyeing my hair with Manic Panic, listening to Liz Phair, and writing cryptic, depressive poetry. There's a long history of white performers earning money while black innovators go uncompensated. I look white and benefit from it. I talk like an academic and I'm asked to deliver paying speeches because of it. So what's the right way for a fair-skinned artist to share her talent, without coopting—what do I owe, to whom, and in what coin can I pay? It's a question that feels more important and more difficult every year.

Doug had to head home but wanted to make sure I'd be

seeing the show at the Maple Leaf. He pointed to a handsome, older black man down the bar in finely framed glasses. "That's the legendary George Porter Jr.," he said, "of the Meters." The legend looked over, and I gave a shy wave. I felt a little bloom of teenage excitement—a bunch of classic hip-hop tracks sampled the Meters. In present company, sushi suddenly felt like a perfectly New Orleanian meal. I leisurely finished my salmon roll at the time of night I'd usually be counting into microphones.

Ninety minutes later, the Maple Leaf was full and moving. I wallflowered with a bottle of beer. There were people who couldn't keep time, people who could really dance, and jazz dudes who could keep time so well, and in such complicated subdivisions, that it just *looked* like they couldn't dance. My corner of the floor was populated by tourists in Velcro sandals, club girls in banging four-inch heels, a slim woman in suede loafers, a middle-aged guy dancing in hiking shoes. That seemed like an unusually wide array of footwear at a concert; I pretended to drop my pen to get a better look. *This club is like Noah's ark from the ankle down,* I thought. Shoes are flags of cultural membership; shows I'd been to were usually dominated by black boots and Vans—hipster standard issue. But maybe a city run by pirates, psychics, and jazz gods didn't have much use for hipsters; there was no mainstream to rail against.

The keyboardist tapped the side of his rig and shot a glance to the back of the room. My reflex was to jog to the sound-board: *Can we get more keys in the monitors?* But of course this was not my show—and the musicians onstage were the last people to need an intermediary.

During his solo, the drummer's sticks moved faster than the flash rate of the LED stage lights. They blurred, becoming two arcs of blonde wood at his sides, like the wings of a snow angel.

At this time of night, I'd usually be onstage myself, just a few songs into the evening. I'd have a mic in my right hand, a whiskey at my feet, and I'd be just starting to get airborne— moved by the music, along with everyone else. I haven't always been a strong performer, but I've become one: I know how an arched eyebrow can color a phrase, how an outstretched arm can widen my presence on a large stage, how a crowd can be deputized to stop a fight peacefully, how long to pause after a joke (if you don't allow time for the laugh to take form, you'll snuff it out with your next line). I can sense the perimeter of the spotlight, and I know that if I leave that coin of light, the people in the back cannot see my facial expressions and their attention will turn to the next brightest point onstage. And I know when it's time to let it all go, and just sing, however it might look.

Outside the Maple Leaf, a hard rain started. I stood under the awning outside to watch it come down and catch some secondhand smoke. The first notes of a slow song reeled people back inside, leaving conversations and cigarettes half-finished. I followed. There's a trick you might have seen before, where a rowdy musician plays a sad song in the middle of a set. And because the scale in your heart has already been calibrated to the ruckus, the weighing pan will spring up in those quiet moments, painfully light. And your throat will hurt, constricted by the intensity of a feeling you hadn't known to brace for.

No place wears gravity as beautifully as New Orleans. Spanish moss, tinsel, and strands of colored beads drape over trees, street signs, statues, people—anything and anyone not fast enough to escape ornamentation. Gold ribbons are tied to handlebars, braided into horses' manes, and woven through the filigree iron balconies that stand like sheets of weaponized lace. The unrelenting *abundance* doesn't even feel manmade—decorations pile on themselves like lichen, or like snow.

I met Free on a tree-lined walkway in City Park. Even for a visitor with a decidedly indoorsy constitution, City Park is a knockout: lagoons, botanical gardens, a sculpture garden. The trees in New Orleans grow into shapes that resemble ball-and-socket joints, ropes of muscle, and parallel bones—radius and ulna with a sunken hollow in between. It's like they don't know they're plants.

Free sat on a park bench, wearing camo pants and a jeweler's magnifying headband over his dreadlocks. Reggae played from his truck, parked nearby with the windows down. Beside him he had a tin of green sequins, a Coors tallboy, a soft pack of Camel Filters, and one of those pincushions shaped like a tomato.

"What are you sewing?"

Free showed me an oblong strip of satin just longer than his hand. He was affixing tiny gold beads and emerald sequins to the whole thing to make a feather for his chief's crown. While working, he explained he was a Mardi Gras Indian, Washitaw Nation, born and raised in the 7th Ward. They sewed all year long, making suits—elaborate outfits covered in feathers, beads, and rhinestones. Then on Mardi Gras, they donned their finery to face off with other tribes in the street, "based on who can sing the best and who's prettiest." I watched him work the needle. "This is called the popcorn stitch," he said, "one sequin and three beads. Time-consuming, but it makes the suit so much better."

My mom taught me to sew when I was a kid. My blossoming neuroticism immediately fixated on the stitchwork—I'd wanted to "win" quilting with tiny, uniform stitches. My mother would have been impressed by Free's careful needle.

He pulled out his phone to show me a video from last year. "My tribe is known for the three-dimensional suit." Onscreen, gloved black men wore soaring lime green feathered headdresses, making Vegas look like a farm team. Boys strutted with feathered staffs twice their height, wearing sequin work that boiled in the sun. Those were the flagboys, he told me. Each tribe had a hierarchy with many roles—a big chief, a big queen, a witch doctor. Free himself was a wild man. His suit would have horns.

On Mardi Gras, spy boys scouted ahead of the procession. They'd signal when another tribe was near and the contest could begin. Both chiefs would posture and dance, each staking his claim as the prettiest of all. "It's friendly competition," Free said. "Mostly."

Later, I would look up the Mardi Gras Indians, whose cultural origins proved difficult to discern. Some accounts suggest that black neighborhoods formed tribes and paraded as Indians to express respect and gratitude for the help that runaway slaves received from Native communities. Some suggested the two communities mixed and some Mardi Gras Indians had Native ancestry.

Free said the day after Mardi Gras he was going to start his suit for *next* year. After I'd agreed not to reveal it to anyone, he showed me the color scheme he had planned. I'm at liberty to tell you only that it's beautiful.

Traffic noses through the French Quarter with a strange, slow calm—the cars move like fish in a restaurant's aquarium: too tightly stocked to maneuver freely, but too well fed to mind. If you're heading down Bourbon Street on foot, a dozen songs might hit you, layering atop one another like horseshoes. In dark taverns cover bands play eighties hits; the bright daiquiri joints spin rap and R & B; ragged buskers play whatever songs they know on banged-up guitars.

Every afternoon GM Scoe set up a folding table on Bourbon with two chessboards and a blitz clock. He played there till after dark. Then, he said, he'd move to Canal Street to play until 6 A.M.

GM Scoe is from Detroit, but comes through New Orleans on a circuit, playing cash games of chess on the street. "I go where there's action. Wherever people are having a good time drinking." He's best at blitz—games played against the count-down clock. He had a round face shaded by a ball cap, pretty teeth when he showed them. *GM* stands for "Grand Master"; his given name was Roscoe. Loser pays winner twenty bucks a game.

"Can you tell the good players right away, even before they sit down?"

No, but within five or ten moves he'd know. "Lotta guys been in prison are good players." They'd had time to practice. But, he added, "the players above my level are usually tournament players, not street players."

Real grand masters don't usually hustle, he said. But he thought he'd played one once, a guy from the Philippines. The guy beat Scoe, but then seemed guilty about it. He came back for a rematch and said Scoe wouldn't have to pay, no matter the outcome. It was a fierce game. Scoe suspected the guy let him win.

Did he play women? I asked. Sometimes, he said. If Scoe was going to try to hustle me, that would have been his moment. He let it pass.

Scoe's soft sell seemed out of place on Bourbon, where bar staff hawked 3-for-1s from doorways, the evangelists carried crosses with LED displays, and even the living statues, spray-painted silver and gold, seemed to be talking half the time.

I hadn't played chess in years—I tried to make a quick appraisal of my current skill level. Did I remember how all the pieces moved? I did. Unbidden, the term *castle* rose to mind, which irritated me because castling is an exotic move that's rarely necessary but is a favorite of know-it-alls who parade the term about to demonstrate their savvy. If I were to sit down at Scoe's table, could I put up any sort of strategy? I doubted it. My dad taught me to play when I was a girl; he had a tiny electronic board that allowed him to face off against the machine, frowning down at the petite grid. Each piece was the size of a tooth and had to be pressed until a beep indicated the computer knew what you'd done. In retrospect, it seems strange to think that he bought a beeping toy to play a social game alone.

I knew that I was probably bad for business. Occupied in conversation with me, Scoe couldn't properly hail paying customers. I left him to his work on Bourbon, hoping some drunk out-of-towner would stumble up with money to lose.

In New Orleans, the Mississippi winds like a cursive word that's just been pulled too straight to decipher. My last morning in town, I set my alarm for 6:20 to watch the sunrise over the water—I hadn't seen a sunrise in any city in a long time. I sat on the steps of a riverbank pavilion. A crescent moon was still in the sky. A crew of men worked a high crane, as if they'd just hung it there.

The sun came up faster than I expected, jogging through a metal spectrum—bronze, copper, rose gold—before dialing into daylight.

I left the riverbank to head back into the French Quarter. With the sun still low behind me, my shadow was the tallest I could remember seeing it. Sixty-five feet—I estimated by counting the steps it took to walk the length of her.

Touring with my rap crew, I'm usually in the company of six or seven men. And between those tours, I often travel overseas alone. Maneuvering as a single foreigner is a task that occupies my whole brain, leaving it no time to generate the usual din of anxious chatter. The signage with strange letters, the thousand ways that dark-haired women fix their scarves, the coinage with unfamiliar heroes—it all rinses out my head and fills it up instead with awe and fear and wonder, the way a bartender will wash a glass in absinthe to mix a Sazerac.

New Orleans was clearly a vacation destination for couples— scores of them stood in the French Quarter looking at fountains and at their paper maps and at the photo they just took of each other. I know people normally take big trips with romantic partners, but I've rarely done it—and I've wondered if it might be too late to learn how. I'm too accustomed to maneuvering through crowded streets solo, looking for the openings just wide enough to accommodate my one set of shoulders. It's like when my dad, who is an accordion player, tries to play something on my Casio keyboard. He has to set it on the carpet and lay his head down beside it to simulate his vantage point of looking down the accordion's keys. He just doesn't have any practice the regular way.

At midmorning, I set out for a silver shop on Chartres Street. I've made a little pilgrimage to this shop to admire a particular necklace every time I've performed nearby. It's made out of tiny interlocking chains, so fine that the whole thing drapes like heavy fabric around the display neck—not native behavior for metal. The shop was usually bolted down for the night by the time I arrived. But I could still look in through the glass.

On first sight I knew this necklace would never pass the rap test: Doomtree sets are two hours of jumping, sweating, and bodychecking—both accidental and intentional. I've had bra clasps fail mid-show, inseams give way, and solid metal bracelets snap, ensnared in another rapper's mic cord. But I'd resolved that if I found the store open, I'd buy this necklace. And I'd commit to finding an occasion to wear it: a neighboring universe where I enjoyed cocktails in moderation and could walk down stairs in high heels.

I didn't want to creep out the sales lady, but couldn't manage to contain myself: "I've been visiting this necklace for seven years." She was unfazed, said it was one of the few pieces they had more than one of in stock. In my hands, it was heavier than I expected. Maybe gravity in New Orleans pulled harder on beautiful things. After she'd boxed it, I took a picture of the empty display window, feeling strange that on the next pass through town, I wouldn't be coming back.

Household Magnets

Mayo Clinic is a world-famous hospital in Rochester, Minnesota. Foreign leaders go there for discreet, pioneering treatments. Their frenzied press teams, meanwhile, loudly insist that it's just a checkup—all very routine.

I was asked to give an eighteen-minute speech at Mayo, as part of a health care conference. My job was to talk about life as an indie musician, hopefully sparking some cross-disciplinary insights. Then I'd sing two songs at a roomful of seated physicians and administrators before their dinner break.

I practiced my PowerPoint presentation on the plane from New York. It had pictures I'd taken from stage, a Dolly Parton song, and all sorts of clever parallels between doctors and rappers. I was going to slay and I knew it. The flight landed on time in Minneapolis; I'd stay there for the night, then drive an hour and a half south to Rochester in the morning.

I grew up in Minneapolis and it's the city in which my X still lives. Although we hadn't spent any real time together in months, he wrote asking if I'd like to have coffee. Social media, I'd presumed, had alerted him to the fact that I was in town.

I knew the correct answer was *no*. I wrote *yes*. But I suggested we meet at the chaste hour of 10 A.M., before my sound check at Mayo.

The conference organizers didn't know it when they invited me, but before making music full-time, I'd worked as a medical technical writer. I'd been into biological science since I was a kid; learning about the fundamental nature of things had always seemed more interesting than the sort of stuff we studied in history classes—tectonic plates just seem truer than nation states. Out of college, when I got the writing gig, my first job was to draft a guide on pacemaker implantation.

Waitressing is the more traditional part-time gig for young artists, but I wasn't very good at it. Successful servers have a shelf full of clocks in their head—like the wall at the airport that shows local time in Paris, Tokyo, and New York. They know when Table 1 needs another round; when to drop dessert menus at 7; when to interrupt the efforts of the gentleman at the bar who is creeping out the female patron beside him. But I never got it all synced right. Everyone in my section was always waiting for something; I had to dial the charm to eleven to compensate for the fact that they were all still hungry. I earned decent tips, but my table turn was awful and the constant soft-shoe was exhausting, even for a twenty-one-year-old. I was never gonna make varsity. I needed another job that paid well, but that I could quit on short notice if I was offered a rap tour.

I interviewed for a medical technical writing position at a diner called the Egg and I. I was nervous. Tony, the man who'd become my boss, sat on the other side of the booth. He had a tailored suit, a buzzing phone, and a leather-bound calendar. He offered me twenty-two dollars an hour. If I'd had a mic, I would have spiked it. I was made.

Days later a courier arrived at my apartment building. It was late, very dark. He handed me a small stack of CD-ROMs, then got back into his car and drove away. My first assignment.

I went inside and sat at the little kitchen table that belonged to one of my roommates—the landlord rented the apartment like a boarding house, installing strangers in each of the three bedrooms. I inserted the first CD-ROM. A video file appeared. When I pressed Play, colorless flesh fluttered and contracted on-screen. I was watching a pig's heart pumping water with a camera threaded into one of the chambers. In another video, a man in a white coat talked about the challenges of *cannulating the coronary sinus*. There was a 3-D image of the veins in the human heart that rotated around and around. There was no note for me anywhere in the package.

From this material I was to create a step-by-step guide for pacemaker implantation. But what was a coronary sinus? What was I supposed to *do?* I called my stepmom Linda and cried. She asked if it was too late to get out of it.

Working under a deadline, and with what seemed like terrifyingly important material, my boss Tony taught me how to tech write. He was always busy, so I learned to save up all my questions to ask them in a single call. He taught me never to pose a question without also presenting an educated guess as to its answer—even if you're wrong, it demonstrates credibility. I stayed up late, crouching over my screen, frantic to submit to my editor by the morning deadline. I read through the editorial comments, flinching at the errors and scared the doctors would discover I was just some punk kid with a borrowed laptop.

The hours were relentless, the stress made me cry. The money was great. The science was fascinating. The adrenaline was a drug my brain made for free.

Soon Tony trusted me enough to let me accompany him to client meetings to take notes. To conceal my age I wore my mother's old wedding ring and a pager with no batteries. When physicians asked where I'd gone to school, I told them the truth—the University of Minnesota—but then changed the topic as fast as I could, hoping they'd assume I'd earned some sort of graduate degree, instead of a BA in philosophy.

I learned enough jargon to get a speaking role in the next round of meetings. Sometimes I'd even go in without Tony, talking to sales teams, and scientists, and the occasional cardiologist.

Pacemakers are implanted when a heart can't keep time properly. The pacemaker delivers a pulsing charge through a wire called a lead. To get the lead nested in the right bit of tissue, a doctor must thread it through a series of blood vessels, like snaking a pipe. The most difficult passage is called the coronary sinus, a winding vein that twists in three dimensions. After implantation, the pacemaker gets programmed telemetrically, by placing a wand against the patient's chest. Medical device manufacturers suggest people with pacemakers keep any household item with a magnet at least six inches away from it. It's not likely, but getting too close to a magnet can reset a pacemaker. For a while there, garage door openers could reset them too.

At rest, a human heart should beat between 60 and 100 times per minute. If it goes too slowly, it's called bradycardia. If it goes too fast, it's called tachycardia (though all the doctors just said *tacky*). Most hit songs have a tempo of about 120 beats per minute, roughly the heart rate of someone on a stationary bike, slightly elevated. I used to wonder what the music of other animals would sound like—if terriers would compose in supersonic registers, if hummingbirds, whose hearts beat more than a thousand times a minute, would write only EDM.

Sometimes I tech wrote at the Doomtree house, where most of my rap crew lived and recorded. One night, one of the producers looked over my shoulder at the electrocardiogram on my screen. He asked, *Kickdrum?* Yeah, I s'pose so.

I kept some serving shifts at the beginning. So while working for Tony, I was a tech writer by day, a waitress by night, and a rapper by night-night. I remember smuggling my laptop into the bathroom at Chino Latino, my tables languishing, trying to meet a morning deadline on pharmaceutical benefits. I sweated through my T-shirt and cursed through clenched teeth waiting for the Wi-Fi to send off a message so I could get back up there and run entrées.

My *X* (who wasn't yet ex'd then) was proud of me for having a smart job. All the same, he'd occasionally suggest I quit—he saw the fear and panic and figured no job was worth that kind of distress. My anxiety was a regular topic of discussion between us. Already naturally high-strung, the job was turning me into a hunted rabbit. He wished I'd worry less, enjoy myself. I wished he'd worry a little more, quit smoking, and start saving. It would take us just over ten years to figure out the gap between our dispositions was too wide to bridge. And by then we loved each other too much—we just kept trying to fling ourselves across the divide.

The morning of my speech at Mayo, we met for coffee. I wore a dress X hadn't seen before. And boots with heels. I did not, however, permit myself either eyeliner or nylons. I wouldn't have worn either at a morning meeting with someone else, I figured—and there had to be parameters.

He arrived before me, on time. He'd gotten better at that. He bought my coffee and we sat down at a metal table outside. I pulled a tin of macaroons, which I'd received as a gift at a recent concert, out of my messenger bag. *I've developed a hang-up about waste,* I explained. *Eat a macaroon.* He reminded me that he'd known me for more than a decade and this hang-up was not a recent development. He took two.

We talked shop for a while: the relative merits of releasing singles as opposed to full-length albums, his upcoming tour, my search for some up-tempo production for a new song. He said he liked my dress. And, to my surprise, it all felt fine.

I checked the time and said I had to go. I wanted to arrive at Mayo early enough for one last run through my notes.

We stood and hugged. It lasted one beat longer than a familiar hug would last. At the moment when it should have ended, X lifted his hands from my back, replaced them, and pressed—the way you might press the air out of a bag to smooth it flat.

Walking toward my car, the old sickness hit. A light nausea, like a kid in the first throes of motion sickness, a dizzy sweat, and the feeling that my blood was somehow too thick, the consistency of expensive balsamic. I knew, from past experience, that I'd pay for that coffee in tears. I was like a walking construction site that now had to reset the sign around her neck: IT'S BEEN 1 DAY SINCE OUR LAST ACCIDENT.

I sat in my car with my hands on the steering wheel. And I found a tiny, hiding hope that had been sheltering undiscovered in the shadows of my mind. I had been hoping he'd propose. At 10 A.M. on a weekday, with no meaningful discussion, no catalyst at all, I'd hoped he'd take a knee. And that was crazy—I was crazy.

That's the last straw, I thought. It's one thing to be lovesick and another to be . . . whatever this was. Willpower alone hadn't been enough. I was going to have to consider more serious measures. But first I was going to have to give the speech at Mayo.

My PowerPoint did in fact slay. A writer in the audience profiled me in *Forbes* the next week. To my knowledge, my crying backstage was observed by no one. I got on a plane to go back east.

There are 1,210 miles between Minneapolis and Manhattan. And still, somehow, I'd managed to get within six inches and reset the damn thing.

How Hockey Breaks Your Heart

I traveled to Seattle to watch my little brother sell drugs. Maxie had moved there to accept a job offer in the edibles sector of the legal weed market. He'd been in the city for a couple of years, but I was making my first visit to check out his new digs; I wanted to meet his people, learn more about his career, maybe get uncomfortably high on dessert. His employer, Botanica Seattle, is a wholesaler that makes fancy cookies and delicate chocolates and little mints packaged in hinged tins like Altoids. In promotional videos, Maxie sometimes played a fictional character called Journeyman who wears a hot pink silk jacket, talks directly to the camera in a *Mad Men* voice, and holds up Botanica products to explain the merits of each one before cavalierly throwing it to his right, out of the shot.

I left Seattle three days later, having learned that I'll probably develop Alzheimer's disease. If that ends up being true, I'm not sure if or when I'll forget having been to his apartment at all.

My brother and I were impossibly close as kids, but we haven't spent all that much time together as grown-ups. When we are together, it's almost always at my dad's house, where we're inclined to stay faithful to the family scripts we've been reading through for twenty years. He is funny and laid-back. I am liberal and high-strung. We love Dad and Dad loves us.

Adult Maxie would have been difficult to forecast as the consequent of Kid Maxie. The small boy had large, dark eyes, a bowl cut notched in the front by a cowlick, and a quiet Zen unusual in four-year-olds. He tucked neatly under my arm when we sat side by side. To teach him the alphabet, I made a set of tiny books bound with packing tape. When he couldn't fall asleep, I smoothed his bangs away from his forehead until his face went smooth as he melted out of consciousness. I asked my mother to put plastic on my mattress so that if Maxie wanted to crawl into bed with me in the middle of the night, he wouldn't have to worry about wetting the bed. When he started school, he clung to me like one of those tiny koala clamp toys that doctors put on their stethoscopes. His teachers and mine made special allowances for me to visit him during the school day. I'm sure other pairs of siblings had a childhood relationship like ours, but I haven't met them yet.

Adult Maxie is nearly six feet tall with a fighter's build and dry, whip-fast wit. With dark hair, olive skin, and a small silver stud in his rounded nose, Maxie cuts the figure of a perfectly assimilated second-generation Indian. Which is weird because we are not Indian. Mom is Puerto Rican, Dad is white, and I just come off as a brunette with a tan. We pulled up one of those skin-tone charts once: he's Peanut and I'm Tortilla.

Unlike Maxie, I've aged predictably, becoming exactly the sketch that a forensic artist would create if handed my fifth-grade photo with the note *plus twenty-five years*. I'm still the color of sand, still tall and long-necked, with a full but asymmetrical mouth, strong cheekbones, and tired-looking eyes.

The eyes—that's a trait Maxie and I always had in common. Children with allergies often have dark circles called "allergic shiners." Even as little kids, Maxie and I looked like we'd been up for days as contenders in some latchkey fight club. In a different era, he and I would have been picked off early by predators. It takes medical intervention and a modern, expanded definition of *fitness* for nearsighted asthmatics like us to survive childhood, go on dates, and have the chance to send a new round of myopic children out into the sunlight to wheeze the fresh air.

As grown-ups we're both socially outgoing, subject to occasional bouts of melancholy, and avid collectors of facts. The way some people accumulate refrigerator magnets or porcelain figurines, we keep little bits of nonfunctional information, the sort that can be trotted out at a dinner party. *Did you know the bit of plastic at the end of a shoelace is called an aglet? That the zip in zip code is an acronym for "zone improvement plan"? That the size of a bottle of wine was initially determined by glassblowers' lung capacity, as each bottle was blown with a single breath? That zebras have a ducking reflex that makes them difficult to lasso, and that even though they look like horses, they can't really be domesticated because they don't have the sort of hierarchical social structure that involves following a single male, which means you can't lead a pack of them anywhere because they just don't care?*

Maxie is hands-down one of my favorite people. But, gearing up for the Seattle visit, part of me was worried we might discover that we didn't really have three days of easy conversation between us. I couldn't remember when we last spent that much time together, without the manic drag race between parents' and stepparents' houses on Christmas.

A few weeks before takeoff, I bought two 23andMe genetic test kits online. I had one sent to Maxie's address in Seattle and one sent to my apartment in New York. I thought it could be a reliable source of conversation—we could compare genomes over drinks, learn some fresh trivia.

A lot of people who go in for genetic testing are excited about the ancestry analysis—they're keen to find out just how much British or Native American blood they might have. I don't care much about that stuff—the preoccupation with charting one's family tree on parchment rings with the same gooey, self-absorbed romanticism of past-life regression. Everybody wants to be Braveheart and nobody wants to die in the potato blight.

I was excited about the traits reports. I wanted to read about the genetic inheritability of widow's peaks and why cilantro tastes like soap to some poor, unfortunate souls.

Buying the kits from the 23andMe site meant scrolling through several pages of terms and conditions. I was warned that my genetic information might reveal unexpected information about my ancestry and origins. *Different people feel differently about this kind of information; some people are excited about these new connections and others take more time to integrate this information into their sense of self.* (I.e., some people are racists.) *Genetic information can also reveal that someone you thought you were related to is not your biological relative.* (I.e., you're adopted.) *You may learn information about yourself that you do not anticipate. Once you obtain your genetic information, the knowledge is irrevocable.*

My test arrived in a box just smaller than a microwave meal. It held a vial labeled with a serial number and an instruction card. I was supposed to collect a sample of my saliva in the tube, mix it up with a bit of clear solution in a blister pack, and then mail it back to a third-party lab in Burlington, North Carolina. The preprinted return mailing label said *EXEMPT HUMAN SPECIMEN*.

I wondered, while spitting into the tube, if the lab tech would be able to tell that the last meal I'd consumed was low-calorie ice cream and red wine. The collection was slow-going—they really were asking for a decent amount of spit. I felt like one of those vipers being milked for venom on the Discovery Channel. I went into the fridge and opened a jar of capers. Something about that smell has always made my mouth water in a weird, chemical reflex.

I sent off my spit for analysis and texted Maxie, who'd already mailed in his sample. We agreed not to look at our results until I got to Seattle.

The afternoon I arrived, he was scheduled to hand out product samples at a local retailer, the Queen Anne Cannabis

Company. (That name, I thought, sounded less like a pot shop than a British warship.) He was apologetic about not being able to pick me up from the airport. I told him not to sweat it; I'd take the light-rail and meet him there.

The sales floor of the Queen Anne Cannabis Company was the size of a junior one-bedroom apartment. An unlikable cover of a very likable Chris Isaak song played on the sound system. There were studio portraits of weed nuggets on the wall, an image of a pensive Bob Marley, and a chalkboard advertising the weekly specials. On Triple Threat Thursdays, the third joint was 50 percent off.

Maxie stood behind a folding table set with individually packaged treats: snickerdoodles, chocolates, pastel candies. He was talking to two bald white guys and a blonde woman carrying a Michael Kors handbag the same color as her skin—Sugar Cookie on a skin-tone chart. All three wore dark blue jeans and an article of polar fleece. One of the guys was struggling to open the sample he'd taken; Maxie reached out with a pair of scissors. "They make us make these things bulletproof, so children can't open them." He snipped the package. "But of course, we're all just old children."

The samples were un-infused; they didn't have any drugs in them, were just on offer to showcase the flavors. The way Maxie described it, one of his primary tasks was to persuade budtenders—the unfortunate term for dispensary sales staff—to pitch Botanica products to their customers. He was on site to strengthen the relationship with the store as well as hand out snacks to grown-ups.

During a lull in foot traffic, I dropped my duffel bag in a corner and swooped in for a hug. New customers walked in behind me, and before ducking out of their way, I asked, "Can I take one of these?" Maxie spread his arm wide across the table, in a kingly gesture of largess. I palmed a few samples and stood aside.

He hailed the new arrivals, "Where you guys coming from?"

"Kentucky."

"Never head of it."

They froze for a beat, then laughed in unison.

Good hawking involves a balance of charisma and credibility: part snake charmer, part professor. Years ago, I'd had a job handing out gelato at high-end grocery stores. I chewed my virgin Weed Tart, watching Maxie's technique.

A pair of female retirees, one with a yin-yang patch on her windbreaker, approached Maxie's table. He explained the chocolates were branded by color to indicate the sort of experience purchasers could expect. Sativa cannabis made for a happy and energized high; indica was calm and relaxed; the hybrid blend was balanced and focused. "The mnemonic device is 'indica: in the couch.' Sativa is more cerebral." Botanica also offered chocolates with CBD, or cannabidiol, for a "neck-down" effect. Those were popular with customers with arthritis pain, inflammation, and anxiety.

One of the bald guys stepped in for another Weed Tart. He extended it toward Maxie. "Tart Caliphate, will you clip this one?" Instead of reaching for his scissors, Maxie took the package in hand and said, "Here, I'm gonna teach a man to fish," then demonstrated how the plastic would yield if pulled apart at the cellophane seam.

I used to smoke a bunch of weed as a teenager, but now it turns me into a paranoid starving person who requests constant reassurance that she is not talking too much. I approached the sales counter and asked the man behind it for a tin of Mr. Moxey's Mints—one of Botanica's CBD products that wasn't supposed to get me too high, just chill me out.

Between customers I asked Maxie about the company. He explained Botanica was only licensed for recreational products, not the medical stuff. That meant his company couldn't sell any infused products *without* THC in them—even if people just wanted the anti-inflammatory benefits of other marijuana compounds. Like a diner that wasn't allowed to sell orange juice, only very weak mimosas. All retail stores, he said, dealt exclusively in cash to avoid running afoul of federal laws, which still prohibit marijuana sales. He was pretty sure that, technically, he was a felon from nine to five.

Maxie's sampling shift at Queen Anne Cannabis Company ended at 6 P.M. He packed his materials into a plastic tote and led us to a two-seat Smart car. The vehicle was too small to seem real, like a comma with wheels, but it was a company car and that made it wondrous. Maxie said that he got to buy it from the Mercedes-Benz dealership and that he drank free coffee on the showroom floor feeling like a day-tripper to another tax bracket. There was no space for his tote to fit anywhere but on my lap. He looked apologetically at the big bin sitting on my legs, the lid almost to my chin. "It's only six blocks to my apartment." I didn't mind at all. It was like riding in a thought bubble.

Maxie's apartment was a basement unit in what had been a fancy hotel. The entryway was impressive: iron gates, Roman columns, and a fountain with a lady statue holding a bowl of water over her head. The actual apartment was spare. Maxie had a two-top table and a couple of chairs; there was a rug in the little living room, but no furniture. He was waiting to find just the right couch.

"I didn't have time to go to Target for an air mattress yet," he said.

No sweat, I told him. I'm always up for a field trip.

He poured us each a glass of red wine. The bottle was open already, but there was no cork—just a sheet of tinfoil crushed over the top. There was also a sheet of foil crushed over the smoke detector on the ceiling, to stop the false positives when he sautéed. I told him I liked the design motif. He pulled out a sheet of foil and crushed over a corner of the countertop with an extravagant flourish.

Before we sat with our glasses, I asked Maxie to cut my bangs. They'd grown long enough to cover my eyebrows, which meant they were irritatingly creeping into my field of vision—and also impeding my ability to emote fear or surprise. He rummaged around for a pair of red-handled kitchen scissors and I leaned forward to prevent the tiny, pokey bits from falling into my sweater. In five or six snips, he was done. He held the dustpan while I broomed. He loved sweeping, he said, because it's like approaching infinity but never getting there. I knew what he meant: there's always a thin line of dust when you inch the dustpan back—that's why I hated it. Maxie's always been more comfortable with big, cosmic concepts than I am. Mortality, moral relativism, that sort of stuff. He's told me several times that if there were an open call, he'd volunteer for a mission to Mars. Even if it were a one-way ticket, he'd want to be part of the history, one of the pioneers willing to watch the blue Earth recede in order to see the red Martian world approaching. I don't fully believe he'd do it, but I still hate when he talks about it. I start to miss my brother the astronaut.

Wine in hand, I told Maxie I'd come with a fresh cache of facts to share. In the course of doing some research for an up-coming monologue performance, I'd run across some pretty fascinating experiments on human sexuality and attachment. I told him how in one of the studies I'd read I discovered that lap dancers make more in tips when they're ovulating. Another study suggested that a chemical in female human tears blunted male sexual response. And, in one of my favorites, researchers identified particular dance moves that seemed to serve as indicators of reproductive fitness. It turned out that males whose right knees were especially active earned higher scores from female observers asked to rate their dancing. Which sounds like total nonsense until—I stood up and adopted the classic posture of A Dude at a Rock Show: hands in pockets, shoulders slightly rounded, and *right knee* flexing in time. *Dead-on, right?* Taking my seat again, I told Maxie that after doing all this research for the monologue gig, it was harder to eke out enough room for free will to do any real work at all. There were countless variables that influenced mate selection without ever making themselves known to our conscious minds. You may *think* you're responding to the fact that someone shares your interest in nonrepresentational East Asian art, but really you're just into his knee.

Free will was already a pretty tough sell for me and Maxie, both science-minded atheists. If you could account for every variable in a person's life—experiential and genetic—his or her behavior might be perfectly, predictably determined. But there are just too many factors to do the math right. (Was she breastfed? Was he cuddled? Read to? Given gender-normative plush playthings? Served fluorinated tap water? Bullied? Made to shower with the others after gym class? Undiagnosed as color blind? Rattled by a fender bender on the morning of the SATs? Recently divorced?) Free will is just the ghost we strap into the machine when the manual gets confusing.

Maxie, who's a big sports guy, said *his* most recent philosophical dilemma involved hockey. He'd recently fallen in love with the sport, but the more he learned about it, the less justified he felt in enjoying it. I am not a big sports guy, so I settled in to listen. He explained that in sports like football, high-scoring contests with highly specialized positions, after a "long tide of scoring and offense, the better team will rise above and win," whereas baseball and hockey were low scoring, had small margins of error, and were therefore innately prone to chaos. The difference between an out and a grand slam might be, say, the position of the stitching of the ball at the moment of contact. He said that something like 23 percent of hockey games go into overtime. The team considered the underdog wins roughly a third of the time. If the better teams weren't winning reliably, if pivotal moments were determined by chance, if an inherent chaos prevailed, Maxie asked, "Well then, does any of it matter?" And if not, then it's sort of a stupid thing to love.

In the sixteen games of a regular NFL season, he said, we know who the good teams are. After sixteen games of hockey, who the hell knows who the best teams might be?

"What about dates?" I interjected. I meant to ask if he thought there might be a romantic corollary—like a certain number of dates to determine a good match or something.

"How many dates to find out if she's a better hockey player than me?"

We decided to break for dinner and a run to Target. *Maxie has become such a thoughtful, clever conversationalist,* I thought. I had to up my game.

I navigated while Maxie piloted his little Smart car. A disproportionate number of my most significant memories have happened in cars—maybe because I spend an unusual amount of time in transit or maybe because inescapable quarters provide a natural setting for dramatic action.

As I remember it, Maxie's first independent opinion was formulated in the back seat of a parked car. We were alone, probably waiting for Mom to come out of Walgreens or the bank or the grocery store. He could talk, but was small, still in a car seat. Following some fiendish kid impulse, I opened a catalog and pointed to a scantily clad woman in an advertisement. That's a *Sexy Lady,* I said. Can you say *Sexy Lady?* He could, and I was satisfied by the corruption. We waited some more, making whatever sort of conversation is made by an eight-year-old girl and a three-year-old boy. Then a song came on the radio and I said I liked it. Maxie said he did not. I turned to him, confused. *I just told him it was a good song. Where could he have learned not to like it?*

Numbers flashed on the dash of Maxie's Smart car. "Holy shit, does this thing get a hundred miles to the gallon?" I asked. "Only on the highway," Maxie said. We missed our exit—a shared failure—and traded romantic updates while rerouting. He was in the trenches of a passing crush but had no long-term prospects. I was still wading through the same emotional porridge with *X.*

I'd have guessed Maxie would have had a kid by now, even if accidentally. He's handsome, chatty, generally well received by women. I'm not especially eager to suit up as an aunt, but the prospect of him never having a family makes me uneasy—the astronaut thing again: I just don't like imagining him out there all on his own. On the frontage road to Target, he might have been thinking the same thing about me. But I doubted it. Between the two of us, I'm the worrier; Maxie tends to experience his anxiety in the present tense and leave the future to itself.

Since I was the one who'd be sleeping on it, I insisted on picking up the tab for the air mattress. He bought a towel, because he didn't have any extras at home.

We ate sushi at a spot in his neighborhood then drank too much at the cocktail bar next door. Maxie, when he is drunk, repeats himself. I, when I am drunk, forget parts of the evening. A conveniently matched pair.

For the next three days, Maxie let me tag along everywhere he went. We Ubered to one of his work events downtown: an invite-only industry party with an open bar, an impressive dessert table, and some pretty unimpressive dancing to the music of Ginuwine. We toured the Botanica facilities, which felt like a Willy Wonka adaptation rendered more adult by the addition of intoxicants and nondisclosure agreements. Early one evening, I took half of a CBD mint and fell asleep twenty minutes later, presumably enjoying a neck-down high while fast asleep on my air mattress.

It was over a couple of afternoon beers that we'd sat down to begin comparing genomes. We set up on a sunny table at a place called Whisky Bar. I was outrageously excited. Maxie was sporting. As we logged on to the site, I asked, "Have you already run the scenario in your head where Mom has to tell us we're from dif—"

"Oh, absolutely."

We entered our respective log-in information and waited on the Wi-Fi.

"Who has the Y chromosome again?"

"You do."

A menu of reports appeared at the top of the page. Even the ancestry stuff turned out to be fascinating. There were color-coded maps and interactive chromosome diagrams and I wanted to nominate the website designer for whatever sort of award website designers get. The top line of my screen said that I was 12.9 percent Iberian; Maxie's top line, however, was 14.9 percent French and German. In fact, everything seemed a little different; he had Ashkenazic blood, I was a teensy bit Sardinian. In unison, we navigated to the FAQ page.

"Huh."

"Huh."

Turns out siblings share only about 50 percent of their DNA, because each inherits different portions of the parents' genes. My allotment from Mom might feature more of *her* mother's DNA than what Maxie got. In that way, our ancestry diverged. I had more sub-Saharan genes, which I'm pretty sure we both thought made me the winner.

I was ready to move on to our next report, but his screen displayed something mine didn't. I hadn't noticed as much when we signed on, but Maxie had elected to receive information about his genetic health risks. I'd passed on mine—genetic health risks do not a dinner party hero make. But I'd watched over his shoulder as he clicked through.

Alzheimer's disease is characterized by memory loss, cognitive decline, and personality changes. Late-onset Alzheimer's disease is the most common form of Alzheimer's disease, developing after age 65.

Maxwell, you have one copy of the ε4 variant we tested.

With one variant in the APOE gene, the site said Maxie's chance of developing Alzheimer's disease by age seventy-five was 4–7 percent. By eighty-five, his chances were 20–23 percent.

"I feel better actually," he said. Two of our grandparents

had shown symptoms of the disease, and given that fact, his numbers did seem fairly low.

Catalyzed by Maxie's results, I navigated through my own profile, back to the health risks section. He looked over my shoulder as I unclicked the button beside *I do not want to see my health results,* and clicked *I do.*

When I know I'm making a bad choice, I do it as fast as I can—I eat all of the ice cream before my better judgment can intervene to take away my spoon. I clicked Continue.

Dessa, you have two copies of the ε4 variant we tested.

If I lived long enough, my chances of developing the disease were more like 60 percent.

I felt immediately sobered, though I hadn't felt tipsy before. It was a new, soberer sober, a previously undiscovered sub-basement. I didn't want Maxie to pick up on my fear or surprise—both now easier to detect after my bang trim. But if there was one nonmusical skill I've honed during the last decade of touring with X, it is an ability to tamp down strong feelings until the schedule permitted an escape to the women's room for a private, quiet freak-out.

I put this news in a cardboard box in my head, sealed it with an entire roll of packing tape, and pushed it against the back wall. Then I put on a bit of manufactured cheer and forged ahead to the next report.

Maxie and I learned how much genetic material we'd inherited from Neanderthals. Before going extinct forty thousand years ago, they'd interbred with modern humans. I wondered how the people of each subspecies felt about the other—if parents yelled about getting mixed up with the wrong crowd, if there were runaway pairs of Romeos and Juliets, if there were ugly words then, as there are now, for mixed children.

We learned blue eyes were only ten thousand years old. I tried to imagine what it would have been like to see the first pair, like meeting someone who glowed in the dark, or bled seawater.

Maxie could smell the asparagus metabolite in his pee—I didn't even know that was a thing. The site said some people don't produce the chemical and some people just can't detect it, so I wasn't sure which group I fell into.

"What does it smell like?"

"It smells like asparagus."

It is commonly thought that cleft chins result from an incomplete fusion of the bones of the jaw during fetal development.

I leaned back, surprised. "Whoa, it's a *bone* thing?"

"I just thought it was a meat thing."

"Me too."

Dessa, based on your genetics, you're likely to move more than average during sleep. Thirteen movements per hour was the norm; I was probably batting sixteen. I thought of X—a veritable athlete in his sleep. If there were a nighty with shin guards, I would have bought it.

Based on the way our bodies were likely to process a chemical called adenosine, neither Maxie nor I were likely to be particularly deep sleepers. *Adenosine,* we read, *builds up in the brain the longer we stay awake, increasing sleep pressure.* "Huh," I said. "I always thought of alertness spending down, not drowsiness building up." On a click, a pop-up data table revealed that people with Asian ancestry were more likely to sleep deeply and less likely to move while doing so. I wondered if Asian art features less sleepwalking: no Lady Macbeth.

Unibrows are genetically inherited and were considered signs of intelligence by the ancient Greeks and Romans. Women in modern Tajikistan still paint them on using a crushed herb called *usma*.

The same gene that determines whether or not a person has wet or dry earwax determines the strength of their body odor.

Dimples are likely associated with a doubling of a facial muscle. Which, in my independent analysis, made them sort of gross.

Maxie and I ordered a second pair of beers. I had enough material for a year of dinner parties—the stuff was fascinating. But the quarantined box was rattling itself for some attention. I excused myself to the women's room.

I locked myself in a stall to think. My mind has always been my most treasured thing. Even when I am in great pain, I'm often comforted by watching it at work—as it flags the copyediting error on the cough syrup label, or tries to calculate the number of weeks I could survive on the canned food I've got on hand, or notes the fact that passing sirens seem to be in key with every song. (Hypothesis: as the Doppler effect sends the sound sliding through the scales, our pattern-hungry brains highlight the fleeting moments of consonance.) I would choose to part with almost anything before surrendering my mind.

Of course, late-stage is very far away. Maybe I wouldn't live long enough to encounter the problem at all. This piece of genetic news felt like a positive pregnancy test for sex I hadn't had yet.

But then there was the issue of Maxie. Neither of us was married, neither had kids. For each of us, the most likely primary caretaker was the other. He could've been thinking the same thing back at our table. But I doubted it.

When we were kids, the worst thing I ever did to Maxie was play dead. I'd lie down on the carpet and close my eyes and wait for him to come and find me. Remembering the last time I pulled the trick, he would say, "I know you can hear me." And then his little voice would rise and tighten and even though he knew I was faking, he'd repeat my name, threaten to tell, and, overcome with panic, begin to yell, *"Get up!"* I've done a few things in my life of which I am more ashamed, but not many. It was just so *mean,* and I had nothing to gain. Except maybe reveling in how much he'd miss me. Adult Maxie laughs it off—which means there's no one left who could forgive me; the wronged boy is gone.

I collected myself to return to our table. I don't believe in fate, or destiny, or that everything turns out for the best. I'll concede that everything happens for a reason—but only a very general statement of causation. Some lousy things happen for really lousy reasons. Sometimes you hit the stitch, sometimes you don't. There's an inherent chaos at work and you just have to decide what's worth loving as it floats past in the cyclone. I had no choices or changes to make, nothing to do or decide. The only sensible thing to do was finish my beer.

The next day, we went for breakfast at a greasy spoon a couple of blocks from his apartment. We'd made plans with several of his friends from the weed business and I asked Maxie if there was a drug he hadn't tried but would like to. Ayahuasca, he answered. I'm curious about ayahuasca too, but probably too scared to do it. I'd heard that it could have long-term effects on brain function. Maxie acknowledged that the whole meet-your-dealer-in-the-jungle thing was a pretty intense starting point too.

I've read that a propensity for risk-taking and novelty-seeking is determined, at least in part, by genetics. DRD4, a gene on chromosome 11, governs the way the brain consumes dopamine; the faster we burn through the stuff, the more likely we are to go adventuring to get another dose of it. Seems like the desire to try a new drug might be informed by the drugs already on tap.

I asked if using marijuana regularly had changed his sober life. Not really, he said. But he'd taken LSD once, and that might have.

"When I was on acid . . . there's something epiphanic about the experience—"

"What does that mean?"

"Like, of an epiphany."

"Okay."

Maxie conceded that psychedelic insights are tough to

communicate. It's easy to sound like a burnout even trying to talk about the experience afterward. But his recalled sensation of understanding was powerful, and had remained important to him.

I thought of Sims, who'd had a deeply moving trip on mushrooms. He'd written down his revelations, so as not to forget what he'd learned. In the morning, he had a piece of paper that said only, *Water is the key to life.* When somebody in Doomtree has an uncomfortably earnest moment, one of us will sometimes softly declare, *Water is the key to life, man.*

I took up a position opposite Maxie's to see what might shake out. Throwing a kid an extravagant party for her first birthday—which she'd forget the next damn day—seems pretty pointless. If you couldn't really remember something later, then what's the value of doing it?

"You got to experience it *once*," Maxie said. "What's the value of taking a trip somewhere if you're not going to live there?"

At least you can recall the vacation, I said.

You *can* recall the epiphany, he maintained, just not communicate it.

No, you can only recall *that* you had it, I argued. "That's like, 'I know I spent the holiday in Mexico, I just can't remember anything about it, but I saw on my calendar that I went there and I am told it was fun.'"

"I don't think that proxy is valid."

"So differentiate it."

Maxie looked down and shrugged. Dammit, I'd done it again—found myself playing a game of verbal chess with someone who was trying to have a genuine conversation.

I rushed in to say that I'd had similar experiences—also high on mushrooms, feeling like I'd just cracked the code of my relationship with our father, or made peace with my own aging. "I'm just investigating: How much of that do we get to drag back to the sober world?"

"I don't know the answer to that." Even mid-trip, he said, he remembered thinking, "I can't bring this, in full detail, back with me to the other side." But the experience still counted, even if it was brief, and even if he only had it once.

We both agreed that our default mode of consciousness was itself the product of a neurochemical cocktail—it just happened to be the house drink. Maxie suggested that the way the world is perceived sober and the way it is perceived intoxicated— well, probably some degree of that variability exists between people, or even between moods, between days. He had no idea whether the sound of traffic was overwhelming to other people, whether social attention was welcome or harrowing, or what it all might seem to mean. "In your daily life, you have to be critical of people," he said, "but underneath it all, I try to remember I have no idea how these people perceive the world, maybe in a way that would make their actions and behavior a lot more understandable. If they have a radically different perception of things, maybe *I'm* the asshole." Sometimes Maxie is just so easy to love.

———————

That night, my last in Seattle, Maxie and I had a late dinner with his friends. I drank two sweet cocktails and reveled in the fact that so many of his coworkers wanted to say nice things about him to me. In the morning, Maxie drove me to the airport in his Smart car. Idling on the tarmac, waiting to take off, I texted him, What is your earliest memory? I held my phone in my lap, hoping he'd reply before I got busted by a flight attendant for digital noncompliance.

Maxie sent back a video, shot in the car. He was at the wheel, but the trees in the background weren't moving—probably filmed at a red light. The seat belt crossed his chest like a bandolier. He was looking into the camera on his phone, but I couldn't see his eyes through his aviators. His first memory, he said, was an attempted escape from his crib: "my little hands on the bars."

I wanted to know precisely when that would have been—I made a note to ask my mom exactly how old Maxie was when he transitioned from crib to bed.

I asked if he remembered his Cheerios inspections. When he was tiny, Maxie would sit in the throne of his high chair, examining the Cheerios my mother had poured onto the chair's little built-in tray. He'd lift them up one by one and if they were perfectly round, he would eat them. If they were broken or sickle shaped, he would extend his pudgy arm, and without looking, drop them into whatever abyss might lie beyond the kingdom of his attention.

I asked if he remembered poking the satin corner of his security blanket into his ear to lull himself to sleep.

I asked if he remembered the lie detector I made out of an index card; the strange dance he'd do in the kitchen with perfectly straight arms and legs; my game of playing dead.

Anything Maxie couldn't recall—anything that happened before the Record button had been firmly depressed in his head—was my job to remember. Those moments I should take special care to archive. And when the tape runs out in my head, and the spools are turning empty, it will be his job to remember whatever happens next. A conveniently matched pair.

"Congratulations"

Living on the Upper East Side, I still traveled back to Minneapolis two, sometimes three, times a month to play a show, give a lecture, or host an event. But making money in the Midwest to spend in Manhattan is hustling backward. The exchange rate is against you; it's like getting paid in pesos to pay rent in yen. I needed to find a way to start earning in New York.

The process of making a living as a musician in the digital era can be pretty opaque to begin with. The music itself is essentially free—to stream or rip or fileshare. So a lot of musicians try to make the physical album a collectible art object: adding a foldout poster and a bronzed, hand-numbered lock of their own hair.

But the deluxe packaging only goes so far; most pop musicians earn a considerable share of their money from ticket sales on the road. And because no city loves a single musician enough to hear her play every night, the musician has to travel, and travel hard. Every tour stop has to be booked far enough away from the last one that the shows don't compete with one another. Which means each day, a musician has to drive farther than his or her fans would be willing to. If you stop moving, you die. Just like sharks.

We also make money on merch. We slang T-shirts and bandannas and posters and skeleton-key necklaces and tote bags and shoelaces. Successful merchandising relies on the property of transitivity: a band buys blank unisex T-shirts in bulk, sizes XS through XXXL—garments with no inherent sex appeal whatsoever—and then hires a graphic designer to come up with a screen-printable image that conveys the ethos of the recent album, maybe toss the tour dates on the back. And voilà, the shirt is imbued, transitively, with some of the music's magic—it's like swiping the kitchen scissors across a magnet to lend them enough power to lift a paper clip off the countertop. Meanwhile the recorded music itself, which is why anyone cares about the band in the first place, has no role in the economic transaction. Sims, joking in the van, used to describe his occupation as "traveling T-shirt salesman."

In Minneapolis, I do a lot of posing for pictures. I get recognized at gas stations, restaurants, in the checkout line at Target, and once mid-exam by a gynecology resident. When I came to New York, I knew that only a bit of that equity could make the trip with me.

On the subway headed downtown, very rarely I would catch someone looking at me. Usually it was a young woman. She'd scrutinize my features, my hair, then tap at her phone and look back up. Then she would hold the screen toward me: one of my record covers. If we were close enough to say hello, I'd chat and snap a selfie. If not, I'd smile and mouth, *Thank you*.

But newly settled in New York, I hadn't released any music recently, so I didn't have a product to tour, no new merch. I was living off the last tour's earnings, some royalties, and odd jobs: the occasional one-off club show, maybe a feature on someone else's record, a paid speech. In Minnesota, I had a network to keep me busy with those odd jobs. But to build a similar network in New York the same way I'd done it at home—selling CDs out of my backpack and passing out flyers at clubs—would take another lifetime.

I went to shows in Harlem, struck up conversation with any purposeful-looking stranger. I handed out my number to anyone who claimed to work in the entertainment industry. I wrote down the Instagram handles of the good performers who played in the subway, thinking maybe I could assemble a band that way, might make an interesting backstory. I weirded out musicians at their own club gigs, trying to convince them that I was a credible professional—which cannot be effectively communicated by yelling *I am a credible professional* over house music.

Halfway through my lease, I was sleeping in New York, but still essentially commuting to Minneapolis. The groceries were expensive and the apartment was small and dim—I hadn't even realized it was north-facing until after I'd moved in. To try and get a little light, I set a makeup mirror on the cement ledge outside my kitchen window and angled it to shoot a ray of sun inside. Where that ray hit the wall, I hung a second mirror, hoping to create some sort of overhead laser maze of natural light. I went to bed early, wrote, drank white wine, cooked, adjusted my mirrors. I was going stir-crazy and feeling the money evaporate. But my anxiety wasn't really about the money; I've always been a saver and I had enough in the bank to weather a long run of rainy days. It was about pride, and purpose. If I couldn't find work in the city, then moving to New York was nothing more than running away from home—a grown-up on a plane with her lunch box and her roller skates.

Working in the music industry is not like hunting, where you set your sights on a large target and take careful aim. It's more like trapping, where you set a hundred lines with bait and bells, ready to run toward the first sign of action. After half a year in New York, a few bells started to ring. First, I met a guy named Sxip who wrote Jank, which I think is a term he coined for central eastern European circus music. He performed in winter-white suits, playing hand bells and penny-whistles pitched down to sound like a cathedral organ, often in foreign, woozy scales. Amanda Palmer had introduced us casually on Twitter, but both of us happened to stumble into the other's work unawares—he picked up my chapbook at an indie bookstore on a whim, and I stumbled across one of his free outdoor shows in Harlem. He invited me to appear as a guest performer at a showcase in Brooklyn and I read a poem I'd written called "Tits on the Moon." He paid me a hundred bucks and I exchanged contact information with a few of the other guest performers.

Then Matthew Santos called. He was a friend from the Midwest coming through New York on tour. He invited me to rap an eight-bar verse at a fancy hotel party. No money, but free drinks, maybe some good networking. I stood in the cramped basement party, casually eating all of the hors d'oeuvres. When I was called to the front of the room, the man at the piano was Jon Batiste, musical director of *The Late Show with Stephen Colbert*. I was the third rapper to perform. I don't look like an emcee, particularly in a cowl-neck sweater and a cheekful of appetizers, but that adds an element of surprise that can work to my advantage—a Claire Kent effect. After my verse, a videographer documenting the event rushed up to trade numbers; the booker liked me and took my contact for future shows. Jon Batiste, still playing piano, quietly said "Nice raps" over his shoulder.

Sxip hired me again, this time for a circus gig that flew me to LA. The makeup artist made me look like a porcelain Victorian doll and I performed alongside Sxip in a gilded theater full of mirrors and chandeliers. There was a handsome French-speaking acrobat; two almost-naked dancers doing a routine of impossible lifts that had been designed by Madonna's choreographer; and a dimpled sword swallower named Heather who slid a neon tube down her throat that glowed right through her windpipe. Sxip was accustomed to the circus bit; he'd toured with the troupe for years, but I kept yelling "Wow!" like an idiot at rehearsals.

Then Lin-Manuel called.

Lin-Manuel Miranda is the musician, actor, and playwright who wrote the musical *Hamilton*. It is impossible to overstate the extent to which that play permeated New York culture. At the gym, he was on the cover of *GQ*; on WNYC, the pledge drivers wooed donors with the possibility of winning tickets;

online, Michelle Obama said it was one of the best works of art in any genre; on TV, Miranda hosted *SNL*. But even more incredible was how many times the word *Hamilton* was said on the street; that word rang out in coffee shops, on the train, in cell phone conversations. In Minneapolis, I'd never seen a piece of art take over the public consciousness that way. It was one topic of which everyone seemed to be aware and could offer some comment—like weather, or war.

I first heard of *Hamilton* when I was still living in Minneapolis. The production had been running for less than a year then and, while celebrated, it hadn't gone supernova. (Or maybe it had, but Minnesota was still waiting for the shockwave to travel overland from Broadway.) Someone told me that one of my songs, a track called "Dixon's Girl," had been included in an online playlist curated by Lin-Manuel. So I looked him up on Twitter to say hello, figuring maybe I could roll through to catch the play next time I was in New York. (In retrospect, of course, this is ridiculous. Those tickets were impossible to get at almost any price. But I was an innocent and Lin lived up to his reputation as an easy-going, likable guy with a breezy charm and generous disposition.) He made arrangements for me to see the play, and although I'd been prepared to be impressed—by the singing, the dancing, the catchy compositions—the tragic romance of the storyline blindsided me. I wept into the sleeve of my sweater, trying to hide my tears from my little cousin, who I'd taken as my guest.

I had met with Lin a few times since then, texted on occasion, but we hadn't spoken on the phone. I picked up his call immediately, my side of the conversation echoing off the walls of my apartment. Lin asked if I'd be game to cover a song for *The Hamilton Mixtape*. At that point, the other artists publicly confirmed for the project included John Legend, Alicia Keys, and Questlove. The song was called "Congratulations," he said. It hadn't been featured in the musical, but he could send sheet music and a link to a live performance by Renée Elise Goldsberry, the actress who'd played Angelica on Broadway. Lin was in a car, running between events. He said he'd send an email with details.

I hung up and did a touchdown dance in my apartment. Pacing, I sent texts to musician friends to assemble my team. Jessy Greene could record violin from her house in LA. Andy Thompson, a composer and multi-instrumentalist, could run point on an arrangement. Lazerbeak was game to help with production. Andy enlisted a couple of other players and Lazerbeak said he'd start digging for sounds to craft a percussion treatment. Over the next couple of months, we could pull together something awesome.

When I got the email from Lin's team, the song was due in six days.

Within thirty hours, string players were recording parts in their home studios. I flew back to Minneapolis, where Andy Thompson had been working nonstop out of his basement. Lazerbeak came over and opened his laptop on his knees. I tracked vocals standing barefoot on Andy's carpet. I struggled with the high note, tried again, then again. (*How can these Broadway dudes hit this shit while dancing in corsets?*) On Andy's urging I sang louder than I was used to doing; my pitch wandered all over the place as I strained to project. Andy's voice through my headphones encouraged me to push: *That's great, just gotta get on top of it.* The final takes sounded strange to me— my instrument, played by someone else.

We took a break for dinner and I bought Andy's kids pizza. To our collective surprise (and my concern), one of Andy's five-year-old sons ate as much as six-foot-two Lazerbeak. I waited, but no one threw up. We wrapped for the night, leaving Andy to mix.

"Congratulations" is sung from the perspective of a woman who has spent many years in love with a man she can't have. Although she's moved far away, she still pines for his affection, and is exasperated by his infidelities. It seemed I was destined to sing torch songs to difficult men, even at a 250-year remove. I did a convincing cover.

I submitted the finished product to Lin and his team at Atlantic. Then I got busy with digital housekeeping. The release date was just a couple of months away. When the mixtape dropped, I wanted it to be easy for new fans to find me, listen to my work, and connect with me directly on social platforms. With help from the Doomtree team, and a couple of industry friends, I set to work updating my profiles on the streaming sites. (God, was Spotify still using the photo with long hair? People might not even know that that's the same person. And why can't iTunes separate my discography from the work of the other Dessa—a Filipina singer who seems to perform primarily at patriotic events or on sun-soaked beaches? I could only presume that she was similarly exasperated, that her fans were confused to find English-language hip-hop where they'd hoped to find the Philippine national anthem. If I ever meet Dessa, we are doing a shot together, toasting in our respective languages, and then marching on Apple HQ until someone acknowledges that we are different people.)

On the Friday the mixtape dropped, I gave in to the self-obsessed, Gollum-y behaviors that musicians don't like to admit to. Phone in hand, I clicked Refresh for hours, reading comments, counting likes. As midnight hit in time zone after time zone, the release date swept around the world. Theater kids in dozens of countries pressed Play as soon as their preorders were digitally delivered and then they lost their minds in unison. I received emails from close friends and distant colleagues with *Congratulations!* as the subject line and *Congratulations!* as the body of the message. Jaclyn, knowing my propensity to worry about rain on parade days, wrote, "I hope you're basking." The Nuyorican side of my family started a text thread to share links, exclamation marks, and emojis and complain that the song was too short.

The mixtape hit number one on the Billboard charts the first week. Soon, "Congratulations" had been streamed over a million times and was listed by several media outlets as one of the standout tracks on the record. (That fact is probably due in part to the fact that the song had been cut from the original production. Fans were excited to hear a new composition from Lin and his collaborators.)

Once or twice, Lazerbeak and I allowed ourselves to ask each other, *Could this, like, go gold?* Then we'd change the subject immediately; speculation of that sort is indelicate and, historically, an invitation for disappointment. Most indie musicians have a litany of "almosts": the major label deal that didn't quite come through; the high-buck movie placement license that dissolved at the last minute, the rainstorm that canceled the whole festival.

In the end, the song didn't bring as much traffic to my music as I'd hoped. When Lazerbeak and I pulled my sales numbers, the bump was really almost negligible. The additional revenue was so insignificant I joked to Lazerbeak that I was going to celebrate by splurging on a one-way ticket to Cleveland.

But the song *did* give me a calling card I could use in New York. With the mixtape on my résumé, every professional introduction got easier. I was a credible professional. I managed to secure a month-long artist residency gig at WNYC (with the help from a producer friend back home) and sold out every show. *amNewYork* publicized the series with a long interview. My neighbor across the hall stopped me on her way out of the building to say, *Hey, I saw your picture in the paper!* The mixtape wasn't a magic bullet, but it bought me a few extra seconds of consideration from every decision maker I was hoping to persuade.

There aren't many big breaks in music. But I'd spent all my years with Doomtree learning how to work the hairline fractures; a little leverage was all I needed.

My career was starting to rise to the same relative heights as X's. And however complicated my feelings for him, I made a pledge to myself that if I could help him somehow as a musician,

I would. He'd pulled me up and along when it would have been easier to help almost anyone else. Now I was making my own way, on my own steam, and might have the chance to return the favor.

If you can make it there, you can make it anywhere—it's a phrase too cute to be true, a souvenir from an era when smoking was still healthy. (My favorite turn on the expression actually flips it to refer to New Orleans: *If you can't make it here, you can't make it anywhere*.) But hyperbole aside, New York is a big, expensive city, stocked with world-class talent, ambition, and determination. And I had found a foothold, dammit. I might've come to New York to escape, but I was more than just a runaway.

Call Off Your Ghost

Four women play key roles in the following case study. Two of them research the human brain. One of them is dead. And one of them is me.

With help from my collaborators, I designed a scientific protocol to fall out of love. It was part science project, part art project, and part earnest attempt to solve a real-world problem. I'd been in love with the same man for a very long time—years. He had feelings too, but we'd made each other thoroughly unhappy.

Time, distance, whiskey—I'd already tried all of the over-the-counter remedies for heartbreak. I'd rented an apartment in Manhattan, far away from my hometown of Minneapolis, and waited for the attachment to subside. I wrote some songs, wrote some stories, made a few starter friendships in New York. But the love was like a grease fire; the normal procedures wouldn't put it down. I started researching the neurological foundations of romantic attachment, looking for a way to Force Quit the program in my head.

I was particularly interested in the work of anthropologist Dr. Helen Fisher.

Dr. Fisher studies love, human reproductive strategies, and sexual attraction. She gives speeches all over the world, writes bestselling books, and Match.com keeps her on retainer. (She is not, however, one of the women who plays a key role in this case study—because she did not respond to my emails.)

Fisher has attempted to map the exact coordinates of love within the human brain. To do this, she recruited heterosexual experimental subjects who said they were in love. She measured their feelings using a questionnaire called a Passionate Love Scale. Then she put them in fMRI scanners to measure their brain activity while they looked at alternating photographs: a picture of the person with whom they were in love and a control photo. The control often depicted a roommate or a coworker of the opposite sex—someone familiar, but not emotionally salient. When each image flashed, the subject was asked to conjure up the feelings and memories associated with the person in the photograph. Between the pictures, a large number was displayed on-screen and participants were instructed to count backward by sevens. The counting was supposed to clear the mental palate, like smelling coffee between perfumes.

The goal was to find the regions of the brain that were associated with romantic love—not just with recognizing faces, or the act of recall in general—to isolate the love alone. When it was over, each subject got fifty bucks.

After scanning dozens of people, Dr. Fisher believed she'd found what she was looking for: the physical regions of the brain that activate in love.

Reading her work, I imagined my own love like a taproot in my skull. If I could find it, maybe I could pull it out.

My *X* is a good dude. If you've met him, you probably like him. He's a musician with a ferocious stage presence and he's pretty magnetic offstage too. I used to tell him that, on account of his double allotment, there must be someone somewhere who had no charm at all—who lived his whole life without a single clever thing to say.

I understand the mechanism of charm because I have a good deal of it myself. I can maneuver through boardrooms and ballrooms and basement rap shows and expect to be pretty well received. But that trick—getting people to like you a little bit right away—is not achieved simply by administering a small dose of the same magic that could get them to love you for a lifetime. They are different compounds entirely. Charisma is an excellent attractant, but lousy glue.

X and I were both twenty-one years old when we met. He'd been rapping for years and I'd just started. On our first date, he drove me to a bridge and led me out onto a ledge where we could sit side by side. We passed a bottle of whiskey back and forth, laughing, flirting, and watching the river rush below us whenever it became uncomfortably intimate to look at each other. *X* wasn't a romantic by any classical standard— you'd never get a box of chocolates from him—but he'd fold a bandanna around my wrist so that it made a perfect little cuff with a feminine dart that extended over the back of my hand like a Victorian gown. He'd write me drunk and lovesick when he was out on tour. He'd swipe an entire bag of tiny saltshakers from an airplane catering cart because he knew how much I liked miniature things. I, meanwhile, cut up band T-shirts to make him a quilt that looked like blood spatter. I brought him home to meet my family, whom he delighted. At Christmas my uncle gave him a real sword. After admiring his full sleeve of tattoos, my dad decided to get a sailplane on his own shoulder from the same artist.

Soon after we started dating, the guys in his musical collective asked me to join the group. Of nearly a dozen members, I was the only woman. We all performed together, drank together, recorded songs and burned them onto CDs together. I was in X's bed the morning of his very first cover story in a newspaper. We'd been sleeping on a mattress on the floor when one of our crewmates shot an arm into the room, holding up a copy—X's face in full color across the whole front page. We all started screaming at once; I scrambled to find my clothing so we could go out and celebrate.

We lasted a couple of years, I think, before breaking up the first time. The exact details are blurred by all our subsequent reunions and separations, but I suspect that in his most insecure moments, X thought I was too good for him and was worried I might leave. And in my most frustrated moments, I wondered if he might be proving himself right on both counts. I got impatient with his lateness to dinner, his lateness on rent, his carelessness. And I got mean, started keeping track of missed calls, canceled plans. He withdrew, spent long hours mysteriously after work, started lying to stay out of trouble with me, eventually slept with someone else.

Most couples would have simply parted ways, but X and I were in the same rap crew. He encouraged me to stay in the group, even when we were fighting. "This is *your* thing as much as it's mine." In hip-hop, loyalty is the king of the virtues. Sometimes it felt like we were forged out of something more durable than love—or maybe loyalty is just love fossilized. In any case, we were honor-bound. Even at our lowest— and I admit to sinking to some vengeful lows—music came first. Both his and mine. When X got offered a big headlining national tour, he asked me to open for him. Even though I'd called him names, even though I ground my heel into the soft spot of his guilt, he chose *me*. Because I'd just released a record and that meant it was my turn.

On the road, I was angry, hurt, self-pitying—and in love. He was aloof, guilty, evasive—and in love. The reviews started coming in: the critics liked us. We finished the run, came home, wrote more music with the crew, recorded, toured. My temper cooled. His contrition was graceful. We decided to take another shot at romance. And we crash-landed in the same crater we'd blown out the first time: I became a petty accountant, auditing his evenings. He couldn't lift his eyes to meet mine.

In our late twenties, almost simultaneously, we each found someone else—someone who seemed like a more natural companion. Those relationships turned into loving, adult partnerships. And then, as soon as they were over, the old love reared up some laser-guided boomerang ghost. And it made us miserable again.

X and I were only good at the feeling of love, not the behavior. Which is like knowing how to dive, but not how to swim.

I first read about neurofeedback as a treatment for traumatized veterans and kids with autism. Those patients would sit with electrodes on their heads while a computer analyzed their brain waves. The computer would trigger sounds and lights designed to recondition the way their brains worked: to promote some brain wave patterns and reduce others. Practitioners claimed that neurofeedback could help people with migraines, dyslexia, Alzheimer's, lockjaw, insomnia, PTSD, epilepsy, eating disorders, emotional anxiety, and healthy people who just wanted to improve their memories. Neurofeedback was supposed to be able to target specific regions of the brain. I wondered if it might be able to home in on the ones in Dr. Fisher's study, for example: the taproot that kept me in love.

I was skeptical, though, of anything billed as a cure-all. And some neurofeedback products sounded pretty damn Sky-Mall (looking at you, NeuroSky MindWave Mobile Brain-Wave Starter Kit). On the other hand, there are plenty of legitimate therapeutic regimens that treat a wide array of health issues; exercise, for example, can combat everything from insomnia to diabetes. And *all* new interventions seem weird before they're widely adopted. The guy who discovered that a broth made of mold could kill bacteria had a serious public-relations challenge ahead of him. But then, hey, penicillin.

Google yielded plenty of people selling treatment services, but I couldn't get a read on what the scientific community thought of the approach. Was this stuff real? Or were these clinics peddling snake oil to the desperate and hopeful? A search through the online archives of the *New England Journal of Medicine* had only one article, more than ten years old.

From what I was able to discern, the critics held that the technique wasn't proven effective for all the claims it made. Even when it seemed to help patients, their case studies were uncontrolled, so the results could be attributed to the placebo effect. Meanwhile, advocates said haters gonna hate—neurofeedback works, even if we don't understand its exact mechanisms. (Aspirin has been sold commercially since 1899. We learned how it worked in 1971. People have been drinking willow tea, the closest naturally occurring compound, since the Middle Ages.)

Online, I found a woman named Lynette Louise who seemed to be a celebrity of the neurofeedback world. She'd appeared on Fox News and on a Bravo TV show where she hooked up the former guitarist of Matchbox Twenty to an EEG machine, monitored his brain waves, and told him the imbalanced performance of his left frontal lobe would affect his relationships. I wasn't quite sure what I was watching. I wrote her and asked if she'd talk to me on the phone. She graciously agreed.

I asked what she told people at dinner parties when they asked her what she did for a living.

"I travel all over the world and try to enhance people's brain functions. Successfully—I'm really good at my job."

She explained that her system uses simple games to change people's brain waves. On-screen the patient might see a game, like *Pac-Man*, for example. And the gobbling avatar moves faster when the brain focuses in a certain way, generating a particular pattern of brain waves.

She said that whenever we do or think anything, our brain waves change. "When you go to ask me the next question, your brain has to shift from focusing on listening to me to focusing on asking a question—that would be accompanied by brain wave change."

I asked if she ever did neurofeedback on herself, if she'd mastered all her games. "Are you like a pinball wizard?"

"That wouldn't make sense," she said. "Because the point is change. As soon as somebody's good at it you raise the bar. Just like every game in the world." Right, I thought. The point is therapy, not arcade bragging rights. A weight that was easy to lift wouldn't be worth lifting.

I stammered a little while explaining that I was trying to fall out of love. "Do you think that neurofeedback could be useful for somebody trying to do that?"

Her answer was immediate and confident: "Absolutely." She said that falling out of love is a lot like quitting an addiction. "In fact, you *are* addicted—when you're having trouble falling out of love you're addicted to the highs and lows of the relationship, the adrenaline rush, and the whole cycle that you were caught in. Otherwise, you would have just been logical and said, 'You know, it's over,' and walked away."

I asked if she'd ever worked with someone trying to make my kind of change.

"I've worked with people to become *better* at love," she said. She mentioned the Matchbox Twenty guy, who'd apparently been competing on some sort of dating show. "But I've also worked in the other way. As a matter of fact, I've helped my son with it."

"Really?" My voice jumped, like a kid who'd finally browbeaten a parent into agreeing to buy a puppy.

She didn't offer any details, but said her son was almost exactly my age, thirty-four.

I did not ask if he was single.

I tentatively suggested a potential meeting. Lynette did not seem particularly enthusiastic. I got the sense she didn't have time to take on another passion project; her website (which branded her as "the Brain Broad") implied she was already busy building a small empire—books, public demonstrations, a strangely campy video series in which she traveled with a wheeled suitcase shaped like an enormous brain to arrive at the doorstep of a family with a struggling child. One video opened with a green-screened clip of Lynette flying, Superman-style, through a waterfall. Turns out, according to the site, Lynette did stand-up on the side. Also, I got the sense Lynette wasn't especially impressed with me. My fascination with her work probably wasn't any more flattering than the last caller's. If she'd wanted to, she could have a line of heartbroken girls on her lawn every morning.

As a musician, I've got a decent following online. I tested the waters with a small ask.

> @dessadarling: Anybody out there with access to fMRI or EEG who wants to trade an image for backstage passes to a rap show?

Enter: Penijean, my first collaborator and the woman I'd eventually ask to affix twenty-two electrodes to my head to eradicate my feelings for *X*.

> i'm a qEEG specialist working with the most cutting edge brain imaging tech currently available. i will totally hook you up.

The next step was delicate. I had to make sure Penijean wasn't crazy. And I had to explain the project without her thinking *I* was crazy.

Her online bio said she was a neurofeedback practitioner and she had all the right letters behind her name to prove she was licensed. She was familiar with my music, she wrote, had even used some of it while teaching a seminar.

On the phone Penijean had a melodic, gentle voice that reminded me of a good kindergarten teacher. As she described the technical and philosophical details of neurofeedback, the warm lilt seemed incongruent with the complex subject matter: like a friendly doctor patiently explaining brain function while pointing to a model of your cortex that he made out of noodles and construction paper. Penijean was a remarkable teacher, though. She anticipated my questions, and whenever I stumbled over a new concept, she served up an alternate, creative analogy to clarify. I had the feeling that if I were a long-haul trucker she'd use highway metaphors, and that if I were a chef, we'd be talking about "oven-thinking" versus "stovetop cognition." Penijean might be better with words than I am—and I'm vain in that department.

Penijean lived in Florida, but had an upcoming trip to New York. I had plans to leave town just after her arrival, but we arranged to meet before our ships passed. I told her that if she'd like to, she'd be welcome to stay in my apartment while I was away.

When I opened the door for her, my eyes were trained on the empty space several inches above Penijean's head. I'm tall and she was quite petite, a little bit elfin, in a pretty way. She looked like Ani DiFranco, the early- to mid-career Ani with big eyes, dimples, and a figure like a slimmer version of her own guitar.

The first words she said seemed strange—something an aunt might say to you in the receiving line at your wedding. As I stood there in my windbreaker, feeling uncomfortably tall, she smiled and said, in that distinctive voice, "Look at you."

We chatted about New York and about brain science, I

gave her the keys to my apartment, and we cemented plans to meet again. We both assessed the other to be a functioning, trustworthy adult. We were not too crazy to work.

Some moments resemble their cinematic representations so closely that it's hard not to imagine yourself on-screen. Emotional goodbyes at airports, for example. Or feeling blue and finding oneself actually sitting on the couch and finishing a pint of chocolate ice cream straight from the carton—movie shorthand for the blues.

As my research got more serious, I entered the Learning Montage: the portion of *The Pelican Brief* or *Erin Brockovich* where the protagonist puts on a pair of glasses we haven't seen her in before and goes to the public library, pulling book after book off the reference shelf. She runs her finger down the pages, lightly mouthing as she reads, face framed with flyaways from her messy ponytail. *Oh, is it closing time? I hadn't even realized it had gotten dark.* The handsome young clerk/fussy matron gives her five more minutes to scribble on her legal pad—she's almost got it.

I studied neuroanatomy on the train, learning the shapes and functions of the anterior cingulate, the somatosensory cortex. Broca's area above my left ear made speech, but Wernicke's area understood it. A woman had been born without the amygdalae and had never been afraid, couldn't identify fear in others. She'd been mugged more than once, presumably because she couldn't detect the imminent danger. Or maybe she could, but wasn't much distressed by it.

I learned that many of the parts of the brain that were associated with romantic love were also implicated in cocaine addiction, with the circuitry most sensitive to rewards.

I was vivified with new purpose, excited and engaged in a way I hadn't been in a long time. I made a plan with three steps.

1. Following Fisher's method, I'd image the love in my brain in an fMRI scanner. This would be the BEFORE image.
2. I'd undergo a course of neurofeedback with Penijean to try to dissolve the attachment.
3. Then I'd get back into the scanner and image my brain again. My AFTER picture.

It'd be just like the diet testimonials in the magazines. Except instead of trying to lose ten pounds to look great on the beach, I was trying to lose a decade of accrued feelings to get on with the rest of my life.

To get my before picture, I had to convince someone to let me into a world-class research lab, lie down in her fMRI machine, and contemplate pictures of my ex-boyfriend.

Enter: Cheryl, my second collaborator.

A daisy chain of people, mostly strangers, facilitated our introduction after I put out a call on Facebook. Cheryl specializes in human vision, working at the Center for Magnetic Resonance Research at the University of Minnesota. When we spoke on the phone for the first time, I explained Fisher's work as well as I could. She'd already had the chance to read through it, she told me. Because she's a scientist, she had some skepticism, she said, but it sounded interesting. "You're not over the guy yet, right?" I assured her that was quite correct. Cheryl agreed to take me on.

I told her I'd email some photographs of X and of another man—a control, just like in the Fisher study. The control was someone I'd known for a long time, had worked with, found attractive, but someone with whom I was not in love.

"You shouldn't tell me which is which."

"Great idea."

We were both psyched about a single-blind study in which the *researcher* was the party ignorant of the experimental stimulus. I sent X's photos in a file named *Dude A* and called the control *Dude B*.

A couple of days after our call—after it had sunk in that I'd be working with a real PhD at a real research institution—a nagging guilt prompted me to write Cheryl:

My brain, which I enjoy most of the time, might not be strictly neurotypical.

In reading a 2016 study titled "Regulation of Romantic Love Feelings," I noted that people with mental disorders were disqualified from participating because "many mental disorders are associated with emotion dysregulation," preventing such subjects from representing healthy controls.

I explained that when I was twenty-three I'd had a hypo-manic episode and spent a few days in a psych ward. I was diagnosed with something called cyclothymia, which I conceptualized as a kid sister to bipolar disorder. It had been successfully treated by regulating my hormones with a simple birth-control pill.

Cheryl replied and assured me that an episode more than ten years ago wouldn't disqualify me out of hand. And nobody is *really* neurotypical to begin with. A favorite expression in her lab (borrowed from the *Homestar Runner* cartoon) was *No two brains are not on fire*.

In person, Cheryl has buzzed hair and a dancer's build. She's an unusual kind of beautiful, a kind that makes you want to keep looking to figure it out. When I met her she just so happened to be wearing a black turtleneck like in the "Nothing Compares 2 U" video—but she'd look like Sinéad O'Connor wearing anything, I decided.

She was an unusually attentive listener. I got the feeling she wasn't a total stranger to complications in romance herself. She reserved a scanner for the day after Thanksgiving.

Two nights before the first scheduled scan, I encountered an unexpected complication: *X* himself.

I don't want to talk too much about him, because *X* has already been kind enough to let me write about my half of our experience. But a quick description is in order, so here goes. His eyes tilt up at the edges, which I have always thought looks sort of feline. He smokes cigarettes. He buys a beverage every time he has to get gas; he just loves beverages. The charisma that I mentioned earlier—it's nuanced. He isn't the dude holding court at every party; he's the guy the whole party *wishes* would overthrow that dude in some social coup at the cocktail table. Whenever a funny story is told, people often look to his face first, to see the reaction blooming. He laughs with distinct *ha ha*'s, like he's reading a manual on how to laugh, and this cracks everyone else up. He has broad shoulders and large hands that are always warm. He cries when he's sad. He can dance, but usually only does joke moves. He casually studies history and he's got some pretty radical ideas about the government. Although he can get a lot of it, he's bad with money. Same with women.

Over the years, we'd hidden most of our feelings from the rest of the crew—partly out of a desire to keep the peace, and partly out of pride. A tour van is a confined and poorly ventilated space, easily poisoned by anyone's low mood. I often took long sad walks before showtime, sometimes indulging in tears, sometimes furious with myself for losing my composure.

X and I hadn't spoken too much since I'd been in New York. But something small had happened that made him want to call. He explained over the phone that a mutual female friend had recently told him that she was ready to settle down. She was really going to give her all to her next relationship, she'd said—it was time. Listening to her, it suddenly occurred to him that *I* might be feeling the same way: that a clock buried inside me might be chiming. If so, this could be the last opportunity to give us one more try.

I was stunned. This was the call that I'd been trying not to hope for. We made plans for dinner the night before Thanksgiving.

I thought he should know about the project before we met. I sent him a text explaining all of it: the neurofeedback, the fMRI lab, the brain waves, the team of scientists recruited to help excise my love for him. I told him that as an art project, I was excited and proud of what I was doing. But it could also, like, *work*. So if we were really going to take another shot at it, I might have to change course.

I watched the little chasing dots that meant he was writing.

Very cool. Very very you.
Charming and heartbreaking.

In the days before our dinner (date?) I turned myself inside out trying to consider the situation from every possible vantage point. Was there some middle ground? Could I use neurofeedback just to remove the painful part of the love—the resentment, the jealousies—and leave the rest intact? But a tiger defanged isn't really a tiger anymore. If my love for *X* was rendered tame and gentle, I wasn't even sure I'd recognize it.

The brain project had reinvigorated me; I hadn't been as excited about anything in years. My life's interests—philosophy, science, art, the mechanics of human connection—they'd all seemed to coalesce in this one endeavor. And I'd started to really look like the woman I'd hoped to become: an artist living in New York who maneuvered on subway platforms with enough confidence to be approached by lost tourists for help. A few times, while studying the limbic system or reading about the history of lobotomy, my enthusiasm had welled up with such force that it was barely discernible from nausea. And now it seemed I had to choose. I might not get another shot at either the brain project *or* at a reconciliation with *X*. And I couldn't do both.

As a girl, I remember watching one sequence in *The Little Mermaid* with special distress. It's when Ariel becomes human—where her tail splits into legs and she can't breathe underwater anymore and they take her voice away. I hated that moment, when her tail tore in two. Because she'd given too much.

X arrived twenty minutes late to dinner.

I'd picked a restaurant where I didn't think we were likely to be recognized by people who listen to our music. It was mostly empty. He ordered appetizers. We talked about small things: shared status reports on our families, our careers.

Every couple has a cache of signature maneuvers in times of conflict. Some go in for theatrics—streaked mascara and hang-up phone calls; some costume their feelings as rational propositions and negotiate like lawyers at the breakfast table; some compete to be the first to leave the house in an understated exit that demonstrates their restraint and long-suffering grace. The dance that *X* and I do looks like one of those courtship routines of tropical birds: every time one of us steps forward, the other steps back. We're each eager to see the other fully commit before doing so ourselves. We've played and lost this game before; neither of us has an appetite for uncollateralized risks.

I pushed: Okay, so he loved me and I loved him. Well, that had been true for a long time. What would be different now? Had we made any changes that could inoculate us from the old pettiness and insecurities that always undid us? Could he be faithful? Could I be kind? Was I willing to call Cheryl and Penijean and the dozen other scientists who'd been so generous with their time and just say, *Uh, never mind*? Across the table, he looked older. I was sure I did too.

I wore him down. He couldn't be sure anything was really different, he admitted.

After dinner I walked him to his car. We kissed leaning against the passenger side door. Probably both of us considered having sex in the parking ramp. Instead he drove me to my parking spot. He said I should do it, I should go through with the brain stuff. If I wanted an easy exit, he was giving me one. Yes, I agreed. I should go through with it.

I woke up several times that night, tightly cocooned in my own sheets. I wasn't tossing or turning, just spinning slowly, like a drill.

Before a person gets into an fMRI machine, she has to go through a little checklist to make sure she isn't bringing any metal in with her. The machine is essentially a big, expensive magnet. By tracking the concentrations of "spent" iron (hemoglobin that's already delivered its cargo of oxygen to brain cells), researchers can plot which parts of the brain are making the biggest metabolic demand—those are the ones that are most active.

If you have an old-school pacemaker or pin in your hip, the magnet will pull on it. Same with color contacts, IUDs, glitter nail polish, nicotine patches, or tattooed eyeliner. I'd been warned that any bra-and-panty sets with silvery threads running through them could heat up. I'd also been told that when the machine started, my back and legs might start to tingle. I might get a metallic taste in my mouth. When the checklist asked if I was claustrophobic, I'd circled *No*—but I'd never had any reason to stay in such a small space for so long before. If I started to panic, I was supposed to squeeze a rubber ball that would sound an alarm in the control room. I could take all the time I needed to get comfortable, though. It was the day after Thanksgiving and we had the research center to ourselves.

Sitting in a conference room, Cheryl explained that we'd have to take two kinds of scans. First we'd do a regular MRI to capture a 3-D image of the structure of my brain. (MRI images look a lot like X-rays, except you can see the soft tissue too—the folds of the brain, the liquid in the eyes, the tongue looking way too big to be right.) For the MRI I wouldn't have to think about anything, I just had to hold very still.

Then we'd do the fMRI scan, the one I'd hoped would capture my feelings for *X*. The *f* stands for "functional"—fMRIs allow you to see brain activity, which can be superimposed on the still image of the brain the way a tornado is superimposed on a weatherman's map: bright colors and glitchy swirling.

While we talked, we ate fancy candy that I'd brought from

New York. Cheryl had a sweet tooth, like me, and a particular fondness for ginger halva, easier to find in Manhattan than in Minneapolis.

Cheryl had two helpers: Andrea and Jeromy. Researchers weren't allowed to scan anyone alone, she'd explained, because if I had some sort of emergency in the machine, there had to be enough people on hand to attend to me and to let in the paramedics. She made a face that said, *Rules, man.*

We walked toward the wing of the building that housed the scanners. Red and black signs said *WARNING HIGH MAGNETIC FIELD.* Phones wouldn't work if you got too close.

I'd forgone eye shadow that morning, thinking that metallic dust might be what made it shimmer. Before applying baby powder I'd had to Google *Is talc metal?* How was it possible that I'd reached adulthood without knowing what metal was?

Cheryl gave me a set of forest-green scrubs and led me to a changing room. I took off all my jewelry. My fingers were indented where the rings had been. I almost never see my hands bare; they looked like someone else's. I pulled the bobby pins out of my hair and it fell over my face, it hadn't been properly cut in a long time. Standing alone, in plain panties and a sports bra, ringless, and with no one to charm or persuade, it hit me that I was maybe doing something totally insane.

Andrea handed me a set of blaze orange earplugs and helped me settle onto the narrow gurney. Then she pressed the button to glide me into the machine. There was a mirror inside the scanner; when the gurney slid into position, the mirror was inches above my eyes and angled so that I could see a projection screen mounted somewhere past the top of my head. To keep me occupied while the machine calibrated itself, Jeromy queued up the animated movie *Ice Age*. I could see the cursor moving as he struggled with the language settings. While the whirring machine prepared to measure my brain in thin slices, I watched a cartoon woolly mammoth berate a taxonomically ambiguous yellow character in Spanish.

To be totally isolated and also closely scrutinized is a strange pairing of social variables—the ambiance inside an MRI scanner isn't found in many other environments. The tight quarters made large movements impossible; my body trusted it was safe only because my mind constantly cooed and patted and murmured reassurances. The cheap earplugs dampened treble more effectively than bass and the world melted into a low-register slurry. I wonder if being scanned might be a *tiny* bit like being an astronaut: you're tethered to the human world, but far removed from its daily business, afforded a vantage point that is rare and modern and only just barely on this side of possible. But instead of watching the blue Earth, rising as a crescent in the dark, you're providing a view of the contents of your own helmet, your own skull—a view of the very entity doing all the viewing.

After the first scans, Cheryl's voice came over the crackling intercom, "You have a beautiful brain."

"I bet you say that to all your subjects."

"Yeah. But sometimes I mean it."

———————

The strength of a magnet is measured in units called teslas. I did my structural scan in a 3T scanner. I'd do the fMRI scanning in a 7T machine. As the magnetic field strength increases, so does the resolution of the image that can be produced. The stronger the magnet, however, the more oppressive the confines of the scanner: the tunnel into which the body slides is longer. A circle of light past the tips of one's toes is the only portal to the known world.

The 7T rig took up a whole room. It was shaped like a Little Debbie Swiss Roll, but as big as a truck. I would be inserted as the center swirl of frosting. Even when it wasn't scanning, the 7T was loud. It didn't hum like a normal, idling machine; it chirped and squeaked like an aviary whose birds were all hidden in the foliage. Andrea said that was the helium coolant system, which ran 24/7.

I lay down on the gurney. Andrea tucked blankets around me and slid a foam prop under my knees. An irrational, powerful affection for her swept through me—like a soldier falling for the nurse. This time she fitted a panel over the top half of my face. It had eyeholes, like a Batman mask.

She pressed the button that slid me into the machine, headfirst. My vision started to jog and drift. The world began to wind clockwise.

Over the intercom: "You okay?"

"Just—just got the spins."

Did my voice sound like a person about to throw up? I did not think that it did. I shut my eyes. I didn't know it yet, but every 7T scan would be like this: clockwise going in; counter-clockwise coming out. I was a hairspring.

My brain swirled in smaller circles, then landed, like a leaf. I opened my eyes. The space was so small. Even if I freaked out, I wouldn't know how to wriggle free—my face would hit the quarter-million-dollar Batman mask even before my head hit the scanner walls. It was loud inside and I was glad; I didn't want to hear my own breathing.

A voice came over the intercom. "Ready?"

"Yes."

Small white text appeared: *Noise coming.* Ticks, a loud bang-ing, and a sustained buzz rose up around me. It was like being buried alive in a fax machine. The first image flashed, a photo-graph of a face that I knew very well. A familiar surge of love and pain washed through me.

When I am standing barefoot, my heart is about 56 inches off the ground. When Cheryl is standing barefoot, her bottom lip is 56 inches off the floor. When Penijean is barefoot, her ears are 56 inches off the ground.

The shapes and sizes of brains are variable too. If a neurolo-gist inserted a 56-millimeter probe through the tops of our heads, she might end up in different parts of our brains.

To navigate their patients' anatomy accurately, neurolo-gists rely on brain atlases. Imagine a system of latitude and lon-gitude, but that the grid sinks all the way to the core. The seminal brain atlas was created by a guy named Jean Talairach in 1967 at Centre Hospitalier Sainte-Anne in Paris. He dissected a human brain, plotting the exact location of every structure on a three-dimensional grid. The amygdala, the hippocampus, the thalamus—he could now provide precise coordinates for all of them. To use the valuable information Talairach collected, neurologists today rescale the images of their patients' brains to fit the one that he dissected—the same way you might move a projector closer or farther from a screen to get the image to fill it entirely.

Enter: my third and final collaborator, the woman Talairach dissected.

In the days after my scans, my data was mapped to her brain. The process involved warping the images so that my skull didn't look quite like my own anymore. Cheryl said the dissected brain had been sitting on a table for a while, so it sort of sagged. I imagined Greenland and Iceland—the parts of the globe most distended by Mercator's rolling pin.

I wanted to know more about the woman whose brain became the standard model. But even after a sustained search, conducted in both English and clumsy French, I couldn't find much of anything. She was sixty years old, probably Parisian. Smallish head, smallish brain. Likely an alcoholic. Had she known she was dying when she decided to donate her brain? Or could a son or daughter have made the decision for her? I wondered if she was in love when she died. I presumed a small head can hold just as much love as a standard one. Or maybe relatively more, I thought, if the love is standard sized and the head is small.

Research subjects are often anonymized in scientific literature, known only as Mr. R or M—or some other veiled handle. But I wondered if enough time had passed for the identity of Talairach's subject to be revealed. The doctor himself was dead; I read his obit in *Le Monde*. I couldn't find a living widow, but I contacted a doctor at Harvard who had studied under him. The doctor didn't know anything about the dissected woman, but wrote me to reiterate that Talairach's work had revolutionized his field.

She would have seen both world wars. Probably, she would have fallen in love for the first time in the years between them. She would have been twenty-one—the age I'd been when I met *X*—in 1928. A leap year, right before the crash.

It was strange to think that so much science rested on her one set of slight shoulders, that so many studies had been calibrated with her brain. I wished one of the articles that heralded Talairach's great contribution would thank her too, or that the atlas carried both of their names, like the hyphenated kid of feminist parents. There were two brains at work on that table.

Cheryl sent an email with the results of the first scans. I opened her message at a coffee shop. Based on the behavior of my brain in the scanner, she made a guess as to which of the two men in the photographs I was in love with: Dude A. She was right; A was *X*.

She'd enlisted the help of a colleague named Phil to analyze the data. They'd uploaded all their work into a Google Drive file named Heartbreakin_DudeZ. In it, I found videos of my brain, modeled in 3-D, spinning slowly. Color splotches indicated regions of activity—as I counted backward by seven, as I contemplated the control image, and as I looked at images of *X*. I watched the Dude A video again and again. There it was—my brain spangled with love.

I left my computer open on the table and walked out. I teared up standing on the sidewalk. *Of course* I was in love, so why would proof of it feel like a vindication? I felt like a patient who'd been told for years *It's all in your head,* but finally found the blood test to diagnose her rare disease to prove she wasn't crazy. Except in my case, I was the patient campaigning, *It's in my head—and it's making me crazy.*

A week later, very late at night, I stopped at a twenty-four-hour FedEx Office to print out a copy of the Passionate Love Scale. For good measure, I printed out the Infatuation and Attachment Scales questionnaire too. I had just played a concert and I was still wearing heels and a show dress. A woman in formalwear at FedEx enjoys a wide berth.

I went home and sat on the floor to spread the papers out on my coffee table. These surveys were designed to measure my feelings for *X.* In one sense, trying to quantify love sounds ridiculously clinical, like recruiting a bunch of owls to definitively determine how many licks it takes to get to the center of a Tootsie Pop. On the other hand, without making careful notes in real time, subjective experiences can be difficult to compare to one another. I'd have a hard time ranking last year's headaches by intensity, for example. I'm not even sure how long most headaches last—it's usually only when someone asks "Is your headache gone?" that I realize it's over.

Fisher had used the Passionate Love Scale in her study, so I took that one first.

1. Since I've been involved with _____, my emotions have been on a roller coaster.
2. I would feel deep despair if _____ left me.
3. Sometimes my body trembles with excitement at the sight of _____.

It went on for thirty statements, and I was supposed to indicate the extent to which I agreed on a scale of 1–9.

The questions on sex and attraction were the easiest; we'd always been good at that.

The other questionnaire was based on a slightly different model of love, one that distinguished infatuation and attachment. Strangely, it seemed both more poetic and more bodily.

1. I stare into the distance while I think of _____.

Who does that? Outside of paperback fiction, do people really do that—*stare into the distance*? I spent a long beat thinking on it, before realizing I was, at that very moment, staring into the distance. I marked an 8.

6. My feelings for _____ reduce my appetite.

Huh. That was true. Seeing that bit of intimate experience there on the page felt like tucking into bed alone and receiving a text message from an unrecognized number: Sleep well. Who is this—and how did they know?

11. I hope my feelings for _____ will never end.

You're killing me here.

I studied philosophy in college. In class one day, my instructor led a discussion on the relationship between the brain and the mind. The collective student assumption, I think, had been that the brain was where the mind lived—like a birdhouse. But the instructor poked all sorts of holes in that idea; how would a thing made out of matter even communicate with an immaterial thing? My prof presented an alternative relation-ship: What if mind were a *function* of brain? My mind was blown. My brain remained intact.

Very casually, I started jotting down a few of my own pet theories. What if brain is to mind as hand is to fist? Like, maybe the mind is something that the brain can make of itself, a posture it can hold. We have a lap when we sit down, but not when we stand—even though we always have legs. We always have a brain but only have a mind when we're conscious or dreaming, and not when we're in surgery or dead.

I was trying to change my brain to change my mind. If I could successfully modify the hand, maybe the fist would let go.

Not all of my friends were excited about the project. I spent a lot of time confirming that I had already seen the movie *Eternal Sunshine of the Spotless Mind*. Some friends thought that—even if I was going to get weird and sciencey about it—I was looking in the wrong place. Love wouldn't live in the brain.

But being able to image love in the brain wouldn't mean that love is an intellectual phenomenon. It wouldn't mean that it was housed there, not discretely anyway. It just means that the brain participates in love in an observable, recognizable way. I can take a man's pulse by putting two fingers against his neck or along the inside of his wrist or by putting an ear to his chest. The pulse is systemic. I bet love is all over my body too—leaving signatures in my hormones, my heart rate, and my cortex. Body parts don't correlate to specific functions on a neat, one-to-one basis, where the brain is only for thinking and the tongue is for tasting and the appendix is just the screw left over. Bacteria in the gut are implicated in depression. There are olfactory receptors *in your heart*.

Paper Tiger, my friend and labelmate, met me at a dive bar and let me ramble about the project for the duration of a Bud Light. He listened thoughtfully, then gently used the term *slippery slope*. I think he was discomfited for two reasons. First: reducing love to a biological condition doesn't leave room for all the inexplicables of love. Second: even if love *is* driven by a biological engine, maybe I shouldn't have the keys to it.

As a woman who weighs 142 pounds, drinking a Maker's Mark on the rocks at a dive bar will give me a blood alcohol content of about .03. But drunkenness isn't just the biological condition of blood alcohol content. Drunkenness is our perception of the alcohol in the blood. Love is not *equivalent* to those patterns of brain activity that Fisher found, or the ones that Cheryl saw in my data. Love is the associated experience of that activity. I don't think anything exists completely apart from our biological selves—and that doesn't have to make it less magical.

As for Paper's second concern—about playing God—well, I didn't really care. I was too tired of playing sad.

My dad's wife, Leslie, is a food scientist. She probably helped design some of your favorite snacks. But she can't say which brands, because her job is cloaked in intrigue and nondisclosure agreements. She has excellent posture, glasses, and a chestnut-colored bob. She and my dad spend their winters in Florida. They have room for guests and a tropically colored set of towels for every visitor. Penijean and I would do the neurofeedback there, an easy drive from her home in Tampa and better than sequestering ourselves in a hotel room or in my one-bedroom apartment.

I flew down a day early to shop for provisions. Penijean had said that she liked Scotch and almost all foods, except corn in soup—a texture thing. My dad and I went straight from the airport to the grocery store. It was late by the time we joined Leslie in the kitchen for a nightcap.

My dad has a shock of salt-and-pepper hair that resists styling. It's puckish, as if he's always just parachuted into the conversation. He made himself an iced martini in a green glass heavy enough to be called a goblet. It was the only one like it in the house, purchased for fifty cents at a thrift store. He's always been particular about glassware.

Leaning against the sink, with his thinking face on, he asked questions about Penijean's visit. I wasn't totally sure how it was going to go, I said. I regurgitated all I'd learned about fMRIs, biofeedback, and neurological anatomy. But really, I just knew she was going to hook a bunch of wires to my head to try and change my brain waves. The rest was still a little hazy.

I didn't say as much to my dad, but on the phone with a friend, I wondered: If I stopped loving X and then met with him again after this whole thing was over . . . would I fall for him again? And if so, would it be a new love or a return to the old one? Would it be a second round of love at first sight or like an alcoholic falling off her wagon?

Penijean pulled up the next afternoon in a Honda with vanity plates: *EEG TCHR*. She brought cucumber-flavored sake as a gift. My dad told her that she could eat anything in the house and then opened the refrigerator to give her a run-down of the contents of the door, the shelves, the crispers. Leslie had already laundered the guest linens. Penijean said many thank-yous, but not so many as to make it weird. She was good with parents.

A few hours later, I sat in my dad's home office, in a high-backed chair I'd dragged in from the dining room. Penijean orbited around me, affixing wires to my head. First she scrubbed little spots of my scalp with abrasive paste—which felt like hair gel loaded with fine sand. Then she stuck an electrode to the freshly scrubbed site with a daub of conductive putty. The electrodes were just smaller than dimes, each attached to a colorful wire. On my dad's desk, she'd set up a small black box that said *BrainMaster* and had a white circle on the top. Inside this circle was a port to plug in each electrode. The circle, I realized, was meant to represent a head—*my* head, at the moment—as seen from above.

When I was all wired up, nineteen electrodes measured my brain waves through my scalp. There was also one that served as an electrical ground—that electrode went at the front of my head, where a unicorn horn would be—and one on each earlobe.

"Which gender binary option would you prefer, male or female?"

"Female." She typed into her laptop.

"Are you right-handed or left-handed?"

"Right."

"When is your birthday?"

"May twenty-third, 1981." Penijean's software recorded my age to two decimal places. I was 35.56 years old.

The feed from each of the electrodes showed up on her screen as a squiggly line, like a lie detector test in the movies. Following her instructions, I sat as still as I could hold for three minutes, eyes closed. Then another three minutes as still as I could hold, eyes open. My contacts clouded, blurring the roses of my father's rug.

And that was it, at least for the first evening. Penijean said she had to send the data to the Netherlands for analysis overnight. When she had a sense of my baseline brain function, she'd be able to set the parameters for the brain training. Penijean started the upload. I poured us drinks. My dad made tacos.

The way Penijean described it over dinner, brain training wasn't like training a dog to fetch or stop barking—promoting some behaviors and discouraging others. It was more like training a muscle for strength and flexibility. In my case, we'd be focusing on the parts of the brain associated with love, pain, and addiction. Penijean wouldn't be programming me with certain thoughts or feelings. Instead, her goal was to get my brain fit enough to respond appropriately to my circumstances. Our hearts should race and pound when we're at the gym. But at home on the couch, we should settle into a resting pulse rate. Similarly, when I'm in a viable romantic relationship, the loving parts of my brain should engage. But when I'm not, they should, *eventually*, chill the eff out.

Penijean blinked a lot, often while emphasizing a point—it was a little rabbit-like and a little *I Dream of Jeannie*. I'd venture a guess that the blinking was one of those gestures that began consciously and then slipped below the waterline into a habit of genuine expression. I did that with my handwriting: I deliberately changed my lowercase *a* as an adult, and waited for the change to sink in through my hand, up to my shoulder, and into my head where it could live with the other native shapes.

Following her instructions, we drank the cucumber sake mixed with champagne, a drink that seemed native to nowhere on the planet. It was excellent. My dad, a minor Francophile, toasted *tchin-tchin*. There was a good chance that Leslie had formulated something on the dinner table. The taco shells, maybe. She'd done a lot of work on desserts too—my favorite. She'd helped fix canned frosting after Johnny Carson had been unable to spread it with a paper knife on live TV. It's amazing what scientists can do.

A seminal experiment in neurofeedback—the one that served as proof of concept—involved dosing cats with rocket fuel.

The space race of the 1960s was in full tilt. Rocket fuel was already known to be seriously toxic stuff—a convulsant that killed people. The U.S. Air Force asked researchers to investigate: How did the poison work and how could it be guarded against? How much exposure could a crewmember tolerate before it impaired his or her performance? Before he or she had a seizure? Before death?

Led by Dr. M. B. Sterman, a team of researchers experimented on cats, administering toxic injections and then noting the order in which symptoms appeared. Before the animals convulsed, they exhibited panting, vomiting, and, chillingly, something that the scientists described only as "escape behavior."

Three of these cats had a strategic advantage, however. They'd already participated in an earlier experiment—one designed to promote activity in a part of the brain that *inhibits* movement. (Our brain does a good deal of inhibiting—it blunts the sensation of the rings on our fingers, for example, and keeps us still while we sleep.) In this first experiment, researchers wired up the cats with electrodes to monitor their brain waves. Every time the cats' brains produced a particular inhibitory rhythm, the cats were rewarded with milk. Soon, their brains were consistently exhibiting this milk-getting, movement-inhibiting pattern. And the cats themselves— while well-fed—were freezing in weird postures.

This course of feline neurofeedback, it turns out, changed the way that this trio of cats responded to the toxic injections in the rocket fuel experiment. Their seizures were delayed—they'd become cat ninjas who didn't succumb to convulsions when the other test subjects did. Their brains had been trained to inhibit movement, and that's exactly what they were doing: inhibiting the spasms of the induced seizures. If not perfect immunity, they'd built up an impressive tolerance to iocane powder.

In a feat of jargon, the study was published under the scintillating title "Electroencephalographic and Behavioral Studies of Monomethyl Hydrazine Toxicity in the Cat." It was kept sealed for forty years, made public only in 2010. The copy I read online was stamped with *For Reference Only Do Not Remove.*

The next and natural question was: Could this neurofeedback stuff work on people? A twenty-three-year-old woman became the first human test subject. She was an epileptic—a natural candidate for a course of treatment that had proved helpful with seizures. Generally scientific papers don't indulge in much hyperbole, but her case study described the observed results as "striking" and reported "a marked suppression of seizures."

I myself was struck by the last sentence of the abstract, which read simply, "Changes in sleep patterns and personality were noted also."

Sitting side by side at the kitchen island the next day, Penijean and I reviewed the Netherlands analysis over coffee.

Healthy brains activate whatever regions are needed for a particular task and then allow those regions to disengage when they're off duty. The database in the Netherlands had compared my data to the behavior of a bunch of other brains owned and operated by right-handed, female people my age.

Penijean was diplomatic, but to me it looked like my brain was a tweaker spun out on cut Ecstasy and chewing on its own cheek. The multipage report showed hyperactivity in region after region after region. I was stuck in patterns that were unwarranted by my surroundings, hypervigilant. But of course, most of the people who came to Penijean would demonstrate some unusual brain activity—that's why they'd seek out treatment in the first place. She used my information to dial in the settings of her brain-training software, sort of like setting the resistance on a weight machine. We were ready.

This time I dragged my chair just a few feet away from the flat-screen in the living room. I held the jars of paste while Penijean wired me up. With Leslie's help she plugged her laptop into the TV and a multicolored image of my brain appeared on-screen, as big as a basketball. It was pixelated, like a brain made out of stacked dice. Penijean could rotate my brain to look at it from all angles—in profile, from above, or from below, as if we were standing on my heart and looking up through the drainpipe of my spinal column. The 3-D pixels were called voxels. Each one corresponded to a five-millimeter cube of my brain, 6,239 cubes in all.

Colors swept over my dice brain, waves of green and blue and yellow, but mostly waves of red. Red meant high levels of activity. Green was where I wanted to go.

On her laptop Penijean clicked a button to start the brain-training session. A pleasant chiming started, like a malletted run up a vibraphone. It stopped abruptly, then started again. Penijean explained that this noise, this *feedback*, would be triggered only when my brain waves fell within desired thresholds. I'd hear the chime only when the loving regions of my brain went green, approaching normal levels of activity. Penijean didn't use a game program like Lynette had described—all I had to do was sit in my dad's chair and not fall asleep. I didn't have to do or think anything. My brain would learn by itself.

The sound was pleasant enough, vaguely musical. But the constant halting made it strange—like a day spa with buffering problems. Penijean pulled up a menu on-screen where I could select the musical scale of the notes. My dad, who used to play the lute for a living, says that a lot of the piano lines I write are mixolydian, so I picked that one. (I don't have the music theory to know what he's talking about—I just stick to mostly white keys because they're bigger.)

Conceptually, I could hang with this idea of unconscious learning. Pavlov's dogs didn't *study* bell and dinner. Their brains learned to associate the two, no matter what their minds were up to. But how could my brain be expected to change in such carefully defined regions, with only a MIDI chime to guide it? It seemed like a lot of information to convey with such a limited medium—like a game of charades in which you're asked to pantomime the whole Bill of Rights.

The cat ninjas, during their training, had at least gotten warm milk. That made sense as a clear reward. *But*, I wondered, *what if my brain doesn't really like chimes?* Penijean said we're naturally pattern seekers—the intermittent sound would be enough to call my brain's attention to its own behavior. Still, little pieces of a cut-up Snickers bar seemed like they would have been the safer bet.

I watched my brain slowly spin on-screen, at roughly the speed of a gyro machine. When I blinked, the front of my cortex went red for a moment: the electrical signal generated by my blinking muscles got picked up by the electrodes on my forehead. Penijean told me not to worry; the software knew to factor out the motor signal. In her regular practice, she said, patients diagnosed with attention deficit disorder or autism might try to pull off the electrodes. One had bitten her forearm, an experience she described as "an excellent reminder" to attend to the nonverbal communication of her patients. A little blinking was nothing, she assured me. But I'd already accepted red as enemy. I asked Leslie to turn off the ceiling fan to reduce the air circulating past my open eyes.

With a few keystrokes, Penijean could isolate the parts of my brain we were training on the on-screen display. "Anything you'd like to see?"

"The anterior cingulate, please."

Until that point, I'd mostly studied brain anatomy in cross-section. Structures that I'd recognized by their smooth arcing lines revealed themselves as knobby, severe rams' horns in three dimensions. It was like turning away from the wall to see the source of a hand shadow and discovering all knuckles and tucked fingers that had seemed so elegant in silhouette.

If they didn't wear me out, we could do two sessions a day, Penijean said. I nodded thoughtfully, knowing that I would not be reporting any fatigue, no matter how the sessions felt. She also said I could pick another sound if I wanted to, and after trying out a few, I decided on a pizzicato harp-like thing.

Time behaved unusually during neurofeedback training. Minutes that should have dragged passed without my noticing them coming or going. *Oh, we're done already?* When the wires came off it felt a little like stepping out of a dark theater into the daylight, where everyone was walking fast and already partway through their conversations.

We worked steadily for the next few days. My dad and Leslie walked past, talking on the phone and attending to their weekday duties while I sat in the high-backed chair, with a mane full of wires, unblinking and blissed-out on brain harps.

A deliveryman peered in through the glass front door and then went away without knocking. I stopped washing my hair between sessions. I just put it in a ponytail at mealtimes, conductive paste and all.

Penijean and I completed half of our trainings, then took a break. She had presentations to deliver in Cleveland and Vegas; I had songs to write back in New York. We made plans to return to my dad's in a month for the final rounds of sessions.

In my musical life, I was busy preparing for a big show with an orchestra. The harp parts of the musical score, I discovered, became difficult to listen to properly—the tinkling sounded too much like neurofeedback signal. I wondered how it had been for the dogs, how much ringing it took before the bell was just a bell again.

A few weeks later, I returned to Florida to finish up with Penijean. I discovered that my dad had taken up cosmology in the brief bit of time I'd been away. He had books out from the library and was already into the hard stuff: subatomic particle colliders, space-time, redshift, the whole shebang. This part of my father, the rogue scholar, is one of my favorites. Since I was a kid—no, since *he* was a kid, he's been dragged around by his curiosities. First it was airplanes, then World War II, then sailing (a phase during which I suspected he harbored plans to circumnavigate the earth in a used boat). The morning before Penijean joined us, he lectured me on quarks, finishing with a quote from Einstein: "Everything should be made as simple as possible, but not simpler."

When Penijean came, we fell into a fast routine. On my urging, she dispensed with any former delicacy and scrubbed at my head roughly to get a better electrical connection. When the sessions were over, I'd microwave a mug of water for her electrodes. She'd gather the wires in her fist, the coin ends all gummed up with conductive paste, then swish them in the mug like a teabag and pull them out clean. We talked about her life while we prepped and cleaned, prepped and cleaned again. She'd broken her nose in a bar fight. She still rode motorcycles, even though she'd had a bad crash. She wanted to get a tattoo of her own EEG signal. She had a complicated romantic history.

When we finished our final session, I walked outside barefoot to see Penijean off. Our dynamic had been shaped by incongruent forces: we'd essentially just had an extended sleepover at my father's house—for science. We'd discussed some of the most intimate details of my love life—in Latinate technical terms. I waved from the driveway as she pulled away. Leslie and my dad waved too. Unusual intimacies bloom in unusual circumstances—being trapped in an elevator with someone for an extended period might feel the same way: it's gotta be strange when the handyman arrives with a crowbar, lets in the daylight, and restores normalcy.

Back inside, I fixed myself lunch. My dad's known that I'd struggled with X for a long time. It had still, of course, been a little weird to sit in the middle of his living room while a neurofeedback practitioner sleeping in the guest bed tried to fix my personal life with a mixolydian MIDI harp.

The science made it easier to talk about. While I watched the microwave carousel spin, melting cheese on a tortilla, he asked, "What do you think about the project?"

"I think it's probably too soon to tell, but I'm processing it."

"Really? Still thinking about it, huh?" He said he'd known right away—within two minutes of picking me up from the airport—that I was different after even just the first rounds.

That came as a surprise. My dad, historically, has been a serious skeptic. When I learned he had doubts about the physiological basis of my *allergies*, I'd daydreamed about how to present him with scientific proof: I'd buy one real gold stud earring and one nickel stud. He'd assign each one to either my right or left ear and I'd put them in with my eyes closed. Then I'd cover them with Band-Aids so that I didn't know which was which. Three days later, vindicated by a rash, I'd be able to victoriously demonstrate in an elegant single-blind study and a blaze of righteous indignation that *I AM ALLERGIC TO NICKEL* (and also cats and dust and pollen).

But on this neurofeedback stuff, I was the one taking the more cautious position. I wanted to get into Cheryl's fMRI scanner again, to see if the work with Penijean had diminished my brain's response to X.

Leslie wanted to know: Did I *feel* different?

I'd been intentionally avoiding asking myself that question. It might be like opening the oven door—I'd let the heat out and ruin the soufflé. Or maybe the change would be incremental and I wouldn't notice it if I checked all the time. I'd kept my thoughts as far away from X as possible; I wasn't sure exactly how they'd behave when I took down the fencing.

Also, maybe I was afraid it hadn't worked. Also, maybe I was afraid that it had.

I hedged, reiterated my eagerness to see Cheryl's next set of images. I knew my answers dissatisfied both Leslie and my dad, but neither pressed. I felt like one of those bureaucrats who spend all day turning down FOIA requests with the same can-neither-confirm-nor-deny canned response.

The microwave ding was just a little shriller than a neuro-feedback chime. I removed my tortilla. *I have no real understanding of how microwaves work*, I thought. Besides some vagaries about fat molecules, I didn't really understand how *cheese* worked for that matter—making it or melting it. Daily tools, basic sustenance, our own brains—just barely less than total mysteries.

Einstein, according to my dad, was known to end a particularly complex lecture with "If you've understood me, then I haven't made myself clear."

Lying on my back, waiting for Cheryl to begin the final scan, the screen displayed a live feed of the pandas at the Atlanta zoo. Two cubs moved about a cement enclosure, the whole scene framed by the eyeholes of my Batman mask. We'd already filled out the consent forms, tested the squeeze ball, and were only waiting for the machine to make its final calibrations. Pandas seem like pitiable idiots to me. Without help from a zookeeper, half the time they can't figure out mating. What sort of creature can't pair properly without the intervention of a specialist?

Before climbing onto the gurney, I'd stopped Cheryl to tell her that I'd forgotten to change bras—I was wearing one with a metal underwire.

She waved me off. "It's alright with me. Just a little extra lift on the way in."

She was right. As the gurney slowly slid into the small tunnel of the 7T magnet, my bra was pulled toward the ceiling, and for a moment, my nineteen-year-old figure was restored to me.

"Ready?"

"Yes."

Cheryl had queued up the same protocol as last time—photos of X would flash, interspersed with photos of the control. In between images, I'd be instructed to count back by seven, like an Etch A Sketch shaking herself blank again.

White text appeared on-screen, *Noise coming*.

This time, I tried to parse the component sounds in the cacophony. There was a modem dial-up. Then an Epson inkjet printer, producing a book-length work of only hyphens. Then a slow, steady gonging, at maybe sixty beats per minute. It was like a copy center inside a Buddhist monastery.

I made eye contact with *X*. At least it felt that way when his photo flashed. He must have been looking straight into someone else's lens.

In the interest of thoroughness, I took the Passionate Love Scale survey again. But I didn't have to tabulate my scores to know that something had changed. Looking at the photos had felt different—a lot different. Not so much pain, not so much panic. My familiar, bittersweet response to *X* had been slightly but significantly reformulated to lean away from the bitter and into the sweet. I hadn't felt the same adrenal surge, no rising tears. We'd used the same set of photos as we did in the first session, but looking at *X*, I'd felt farther away, at a remove where kindness came more easily.

Cheryl wrote. She told me my brain generated some of the strongest signals of anyone she'd ever scanned. She said that working with my data, it was always easy to differentiate the signal from the noise. Everybody's brain is probably unusual by one measure or another, but that note flattered me—I liked the idea of being a loud thinker. Maybe I also liked the idea that my response to *X* was *demonstrably* powerful—I wasn't overdelicate for struggling with it, I'd been grappling with a Goliath.

She and Phil would need some time to analyze the results, to see exactly what changed between my first scan and my second. Then she said she'd be able to display the data in all sorts of ways: we could view the activity in my brain in cross-section, moving from ear to ear, slice by slice. Or she could make a little 3-D video of my brain spinning around, all the active parts lit up. Or she could even take the surface of my brain and lay it flat like a map—she called that view "the brain-skin rug." But even before crunching all her numbers, Cheryl said that she could see that "Dude A's dominance of your brain is essentially gone in the second scanning session. . . . I believe this is the desired effect?"

At that moment if someone had asked me to describe my attitude toward X with a list of elemental feelings—love, fear, attraction, anger—I'd have ticked through the same set of feelings that I'd had for years. But sometime in the last couple of months, the *ranking* of those feelings had been re-sequenced. Bitterness was lower. Amity higher. And this re-sequencing was not a small thing; in fact, it was *the most important* thing. In the same way that if I told you I was going to anesthetize you and I was also going to take out your wisdom teeth, it would *really* matter in which order I did those things.

Yes. It was exactly the desired effect.

I knew it was possible that discussing my heartbreak with so many scientists—in an effort to persuade them to loan me the keys to their fMRI scanner for the weekend—had served as a bit of forced talk therapy.

It was also possible that I was in the throes of a short-term placebo effect.

Or maybe this little experiment had actually worked.

Before, I'd lived inside my love, like an enormous hamster ball. I maneuvered through the world inside it and saw my surroundings *through* it. Now it was a manageable love that I could hold in my hand and spin to examine: a squeeze ball. The love wasn't gone, but there was a new and overriding sense of benevolence. I was excited to tell *X* about it—maybe even see if he wanted to try a session with Penijean too.

Back at the fMRI lab, Andrea and Cheryl 3-D printed a miniature model of my anterior cingulate. Looking at that little bit of blue plastic in my palm felt like an enormous philosophical privilege. I was one of the few people who had held her love in her hand. And it wasn't a neat valentine heart, it was a mangled pair of ram's horns buried deep inside my skull.

On a hunch, I did a little research on snake oil. Turns out that when harvested from cold-water snakes, snake oil is rich in fatty acids that might actually reduce arthritis pain and inflammation—exactly as the first peddlers promised.

I continued my work on the orchestra show. Harps began to sound like harps again. To thank Penijean, I bought her a plane ticket to come to the show—she even agreed to join me onstage. To thank Cheryl, I bought her a queen's share of halva. To thank my third collaborator, I texted a mixologist friend, What would have been the most popular drink in Paris in 1967?

The French cocktail scene was nonexistent at that time, he

replied, but he suggested a liqueur I'd never heard of: génépi. I visited five liquor stores before I found a bottle.

It was green, like absinthe, shelved with other strange herbal elixirs. Standing at my kitchen sink, I poured two shots, doubles. *Tchin-tchin.* I lifted both glasses, clinked them together, drank mine, and poured hers down the drain.

The End of the Night

After a show is over, we go to the merch table. We sign records, T-shirts, sometimes skin. We pose for pictures and the flashes layer on top of one another, so that when I close my eyes there is a bouquet of them fading back into the blackness.

We work the merch line together, tossing Sharpies overhead, listening to the personal stories of soft-spoken fans, and drinking whiskey with the loud ones. Eventually, a security guard will come by to tell the showgoers that it's time to leave. Some will linger anyway and the guard will have to unholster a sterner tone. Bartenders cruise around one another, closing tabs. The venue empties and the doors get locked and the houselights come up and the truth of the room is revealed: sticky floors and frayed carpet and an echo that had been absorbed by the presence of all the soft bodies.

Our equipment and our plastic bins of merchandise must be loaded back into the van with a precise geometric strategy, or else they will not fit. We call this Van Tetris and only some of us are good at it.

One member of the touring party will settle with the club: review the contract, count the money, and sign the receipts. Someone else will bag up whatever food's worth scavenging backstage. One of us will do a dummy-check: the last scan of the greenroom for any forgotten phone chargers, headphones, cast-off show shirts, or dopp kits. Greenrooms are more similar than the clubs themselves: they are all covered in the same line drawings of dicks, cigarette burns, and stickers from the bands who've played before. Even after this final check is complete, I am the member of our outfit most likely to have left something behind.

Our lives change in the weeks and months between shows. We get married or have children or rent a New York apartment to start a new life, but the shows always unfold this way: load-in, sound check, chips and hummus, stage lights, signing, load-out—because that's the only way a show can go.

Since my last big tour with Doomtree, I have dyed my hair blonde, developed a taste for halva, gone on dates, renewed my lease on the Upper East Side, and recorded a new solo album. The walls of my apartment are covered with campaign plans for this new record: I am booking two hometown shows, one in Minneapolis and another in New York. For the first time, I will tour Asia. Then I will get back in the van for another round of Tinker Bell. I have had many conversations with X and some of them have hurt, but our interactions are becoming increasingly casual: brief updates on our separate lives. He tours, I tour, and our routings loop through the same clubs, like figure skaters leaving crossing cursive on the ice. I see his face on the posters on the walls and I am sure that he sees mine. And the best part of each of us hopes the other sells the motherfucker out.

It is very late by the time the van leaves the club at the end of the night. Sometimes the ride to the hotel is jubilant with loud music and passed snacks and sore voices. Sometimes it is quiet and tired, with foreheads resting against cold windows and phones illuminating downturned faces as we track our progress, a herd of blue dots gliding toward the Days Inn or the Ramada or La Quinta. We pile into two rooms—maybe three, depending on the evening's guarantee.

In the darkness of the hotel room, the breathing of your crewmates is the only indicator of who is still awake and who has already gone under. Eventually, sobriety returns to your own sleeping body, like a boomerang that can find you in any bed in any city and sets about straightening the angles of your dreams. Most nights your body senses that the others are nearby and it keeps itself contained so there is room for whomever might be dreaming there beside you.

Thank You

B efore I rented my apartment in New York, several people
were kind enough to let me stay in theirs, to think and
write awhile. Thank you to Amanda Palmer, Michael Gut-
waks (sorry about the wineglass), Amanda Zantal-Wiener
(sorry about the wineglass), and Kaylan Sliney (sorry about the
coffee cup).

Decision makers at the University of Minnesota's Center
for Magnetic Resonance Research agreed to let a heartbroken
rapper into their world-class research lab. I am outrageously
grateful to Cheryl Olman, PhD; Andrea Grant, ScD; Philip
Burton, Jeromy Thotland, PhD; Patrick Bolan, PhD; Essa Ya-
coub, PhD; Alexander McKinney, IV, MD; Dr. Kamil Ugur-
bil; Dr. Zeke McKinney; and to the generous clinician Penijean
Gracefire, LMHC.

Many thanks to the people in my life who agreed to let me
write about them, including my parents, Maxie, Amanda
Palmer, Lin-Manuel Miranda, Jaclyn Mothupi, Andy Thompson, Aby Wolf, friend and colleague Becky Hoffmann, Linda
Frankenstein, Leslie Wander, Ben Burwell, and all of Doomtree

(Ander Other, Cecil Otter, Lazerbeak, Mike Mictlan, Paper Tiger, P.O.S, and Sims). To Sean McPherson, Dustin Kiel, and Joey Van Phillips, thanks for our many months spent cruising around on busted bench seats.

A bunch of people read these essays when they were still sort of confusing and misspelled. Thank you to Brian Bieber (it's nearly impossible to overstate how much your comments improved this collection), John Jodzio, Sylvia Burgos-Toftness (aka "Mom"), Robert Wander ("Dadman"), Alexa Stevenson, Eric Lorberer, Steve Marsh, Andrew Sims, and Catherine Burgos.

Thanks to my agent, Sam Stoloff, for the vote of confidence and the sound guidance; to my editor, Maya Ziv, who took a risk on me and encouraged me to take risks in my writing; to Christine Ball for the creativity and the muscle; and to Dutton for the chance at bat.

Special thanks to X for letting me tell my side of our story. If you're reading this on the road, I hope tonight's show slays.

About the Author

Dessa is a singer, rapper, writer, and speaker. She tours internationally, performing her own songs and stories, sometimes in velvet-lined theaters, sometimes in grimy basement clubs. She splits her time between Manhattan, Minneapolis, and a tour van cruising at six miles per hour above the posted limit.